Rethinking Weap
Early Childh_ _ _

This thought-provoking read invites you to reconsider your automatic "no" when it comes to young children's weapon play. It offers new perspectives on how weapon play and other risky or controversial play can provide opportunities for healing discussions—including around boundaries, kindness, and consent—and create positive learning experiences for children and teachers alike. Centered in an antiracist framework with applications across diverse communities, this book is written by two educators with unique lived experiences of community violence and safety who each share their perspectives on risky play, questions to consider, and strategies to try in the classroom. Aiming to inspire new ways of thinking, instead of trying to change your mind outright, this book asks deep questions to support you in carefully thinking about the kind of play allowed in your classroom. This book is an essential resource for early years teachers, practitioners, and anyone with a key interest in creating supportive spaces for young children.

Samuel Broaden (he/they) is an early childhood author, advocate, and speaker. He has worked in various roles within the early education field and now spends his time speaking and sharing his philosophy on childhood. He currently lives in Portland, Oregon with his husband Perry and their three (very spoiled) dogs Oliver, Baby Bear, and Moon Broaden.

Kisa Marx is an early childhood practitioner and advocate with over two decades in the field. She is most passionate about her purposeful role in founding The Play Lab Foundation, a nonprofit organization that provides humanity centering, self-affirming, and high-quality care for every child. When Kisa is not fighting for the rights of children, you can find her with her partner tending to their garden of adult children, pets, and plants.

Rethinking Weapon Play in Early Childhood

How to Encourage Imagination, Kindness, and Consent in Your Classroom

Samuel Broaden with Kisa Marx

Routledge
Taylor & Francis Group

NEW YORK AND LONDON

Designed cover image: © Catherine Delahaye / Getty Images

First published 2024
by Routledge
605 Third Avenue, New York, NY 10158

and by Routledge
4 Park Square, Milton Park, Abingdon, Oxon, OX14 4RN

Routledge is an imprint of the Taylor & Francis Group, an informa business

Library of Congress Cataloging-in-Publication Data
Names: Broaden, Samuel, author. | Marx, Kisa, author.
Title: Rethinking weapon play in early childhood: how to encourage kindness, imagination, and consent in your classroom / Samuel Broaden, with Kisa Marx.
Description: First edition. | New York: Routledge, 2024.
Identifiers: LCCN 2023056980 (print) | LCCN 2023056981 (ebook) | ISBN 9781032679792 (hbk) | ISBN 9781032649122 (pbk) | ISBN 9781032679808 (ebk)
Subjects: LCSH: Play. | Early childhood education—Activity programs. | Child development. | Weapons. | Risk-taking (Psychology) in children. | Superheroes. | Death. | Violence in children—Prevention. | Multicultural education. | Reflective teaching.
Classification: LCC LB1139.35.P55 B756 2024 (print) | LCC LB1139.35.P55 (ebook) | DDC 372.21—dc23/eng/20240212
LC record available at https://lccn.loc.gov/2023056980
LC ebook record available at https://lccn.loc.gov/2023056981

ISBN: 978-1-032-67979-2 (hbk)
ISBN: 978-1-032-64912-2 (pbk)
ISBN: 978-1-032-67980-8 (ebk)

DOI: 10.4324/9781032679808

Typeset in Palatino
by codeMantra

To our younger selves, we did it!

Contents

Foreword

Until The Lion Learns How to Write,
    Every Story Will Glorify The Hunter.
                                    —African Proverb

I live just outside of Chicago, Illinois. Like, literally across the street from the Austin Neighborhood on the West Side of the city. Though my village is seen as a Western suburb, the corner where my family moved, which also happens to be the place where I run my home-based Early Childhood Program, heard more gunshots during the summer of 2021 when we moved to our forever home than I'd heard in the 30 years since we moved here. Gunshots ringing out in the night on the city's South Side, where I called home until I was 13, was commonplace, however, and by daybreak you were also likely to encounter the blood-stained concrete the following day as you walked to school—an all-too-real confirmation that the "block huggers" you knew by name had fallen victim to the streets they loved so dearly...streets that would inevitably reveal that it did not love them back.

As the partner to a mate who has been pistol whipped with an officer's service weapon, little Sister to brothers who have been stabbed and assaulted respectively in gang-related violence. And as a cousin and friend to family and loved ones who have been injured or killed at the hands of gun violence, I view life through a lens of nearly ceaseless dread when any of them has to get behind the wheel of a car, has to leave the home after dark, and wants to attend a party, barbecue, or event, and oh, lord, please don't let them get pulled over by the police! This dread is valid and it helps me to show up fully in spaces where vantage points similar to my own are often omitted from the conversation. Being aware of this lens also helps me know when to step back and realize when I am imposing my personal beliefs, fears, and history on the work of the child instead of letting the work serve its purpose of processing complicated concepts in a developmentally appropriate way.

The approach to gun violence and gun reform in this country is lacking to say the least. To add fuel to the fire, policies led with racist, privileged agendas prevent change from moving beyond rhetoric resulting in no actionable change within our communities, in traffic, in our educational spaces, and even in what is supposed to be the safety of our own homes. These are painful facts that we can only deny if we wish to contribute to revisionist history. Like Samuel, I have no desire to be in that club and will be leading with the hard truth because it is vital to shifting our beliefs on why weapon play has merit, is equitable, and belongs in culturally informed early learning spaces.

In truth, this is going to be a tricky subject matter to navigate. It will be heavy at times, and I want to make room for those heavy feelings to land safely and without judgment. Whether you are like me and had the issues of gun control plague your city and family on a personal level, you have felt the impact nationally on a broader scale, or maybe you have never been directly impacted by such issues and would like to know how to create room for children who have, there is space for all of us here. My only ask is that we touch and agree that this safe space was created by individuals with their own world view, lens, and storylines, who refuse to allow those storylines to control the narrative for the children that we serve.

Rethinking Weapon Play is not a story that glorifies the hunter. It does not make justification for weapons, violence, or harm. This story is about survival in the land of the hunted and understanding how instrumental imaginative weapon play is so we can allow it in our learning space in the midst of a cruel world in order for children to be empowered to make meaning of the complexities going on around them. And that story begins now.

Kisa Marx

Introduction

Weapon play is a very sensitive topic in early childhood, and many people have very strong beliefs about this type of play—on both sides. I want to start by saying that the goal of this book is not to get anyone to change their mind on weapon play. The goal of this book is not to have everyone who reads it go back into their programs and give all the children guns and let them go. The goal of this book is to *help support you in thinking differently and more deeply about the work you do, the reasons why you do and say things, and what it all means.* We understand that every single person has their own lived experiences, their own values, and their own philosophy. We do too—and we cherish those things. In ourselves and in you. So know that as you read this book, we are here with you. Some of the things you read may be difficult to wrap your head around or may bring up some uncomfortable feelings. That's ok! Actually, that's a good thing! Embrace those feelings, celebrate them, and work through them together with us! We will talk a bit about the act of self-reflection coming up, but just remember this: you know your children and your program best. We are here to offer a new perspective, a new way of thinking about weapon play. A way of thinking that is rooted in community, antibias and antiracist thinking, and kindness.

DOI: 10.4324/9781032679808-1

But first, I'd love it if you would indulge me in a little story about how my mindset was changed regarding this type of play:

In one of my years of teaching, I was a kindergarten teacher at an outdoor, forest school. This, to this day, was one of the most wonderful and rewarding years of teaching I have ever had. So imagine it, we were outside basically all day almost every day. We had a little forest with a creek that ran through it—it was really just magical. As you can surely imagine, there were many chances for the children to participate in weapon play in this environment. There was an abundance of sticks and rocks and other items that the children could make weapons out of—and they did. Let me tell you—this made me SO uncomfortable and nervous, and I told them "no" every single day. I didn't want them playing with weapons, I didn't want them pretending to hurt each other, I didn't want the families (or my boss) to get mad at me for letting them do it, I didn't want to make them grow up to be violent—all the feelings. So I said no. I told them "no guns at school." But guess what? They kept doing it. Story of our lives, right? I realized that obviously saying no wasn't working—or I wouldn't have to keep saying it! So I decided to do some reflection on why I was saying no to them. As I reflected, I thought about the classroom community that we had created together. We did not have "rules" in our classroom where I told the children what to do and not do. We had agreements that we came up with together, as a collective:

| be kind to yourself
| be kind to others
| be kind to the environment

As I thought about these agreements, I thought to myself, are the children doing this when they participate in weapon play? Yes, they were. So why was I telling them no? The answer was simple: because I was uncomfortable. But it is not about me! So I decided to work through that. I decided to just talk with them about it. I asked them to all come over and sit down to have a conversation, and I started it by telling them that I noticed that they really enjoyed playing this way. They immediately went into defense mode and told me they didn't play that way. I could tell that they were afraid they were going to be in trouble, so after ten minutes of convincing them they were not in trouble, I asked them what they liked about this type of play. Here are some of the answers I got:

| "I like to be the bad guy" | " I like to save the people" | "It is fun" | " I like to be the hero"

I couldn't help but to agree that yeah, that does actually sound fun. Because it is fun! (How many of us played this way as children?). So I was honest with the children and let them know that it made me uncomfortable, but that I was willing to work through that discomfort and asked if they could help me. I asked them how we could do this type of play and still stick to our agreements and ensure that everyone feels comfortable. Ideas like consent were brought up, and it was the most beautiful and inspiring conversation that I have ever had with a group of children. One of them even brought a stick to the group and everyone put their hands on it and "pledged" to work through this together.

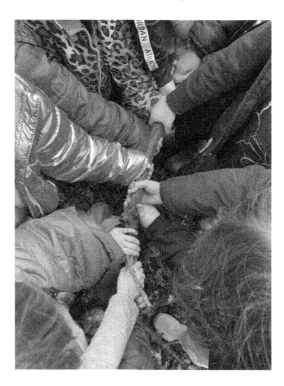

♡KINDLY, Samuel

Now, that is not to say that we never had to have that conversion again, but you know that's not true. We had that conversation over and over again. But I began to notice something—I began to see the children advocating for themselves and others in this play. I began to see the children building a greater sense of empathy towards each other—and the earth. Because of this experience, I was able to shift my way of thinking when it comes to this type of play and I am so excited to share more with you.There were of course other facets to this: how I dealt with co-teachers and admin who didn't agree with me, how I discussed this with families, how I was able to create an anti-racist and inclusive form of this play—and we will discuss all of that throughout this book. But I wanted to tell that story because I feel that stories are important and stories are one of the best ways to help people understand who we are and how we think. Remember, this book is not here to change your mind or to tell you what to do. It is here as a guide for you to use as you work through your own feelings, lived experiences, and work. The only goal that we have is that you think a little differently about the work you do, the things you say, and the experiences you provide for the children you work with.We are here with you. We are in this together. It may be hard, it may be uncomfortable, it may be scary. But you are not in this alone. So come along with us, we are so grateful that you are here!

Words from Kisa

Thank you for sharing, Samuel. You know, our stories—both created through our lived experience as well as those passed on to us through family, culture, trauma and environment—are what shaped us into the two dope humans that are sharing space to write this book. And those stories matter. Honestly, hearing you recall this story about your class was the impetus for change within the culture of my learning environment on the other side of the country. The thought that weapon play was prohibited due to adult discomfort resonated deeply as I was on a personal journey to dismantle all the hidden parts of my practice that unconsciously kept me just off the mark and sabotaged the integrity of my philosophy. Hearing your testimony made me consider the possibility that there may be subtleties hidden in the way that children play, and this made me curious because your girl loves nothing more than discovering the parts of our shared human experience that bask in shades of gray.

So, that is my weapon play origin story, indirectly intertwined with yours. My journey has been met with discomfort and apprehension. I've had hard conversations with grownups and even harder conversations with myself, and none of that has been a walk in the park, but it is all necessary when creating a framework for an intentional practice.

Before we get into the nitty-gritty, I want to formally introduce myself. My name is Kisa, and I will be adding our necessary shade of gray to the process of rethinking weapon play. As I mentioned in the forward, I grew up on Chicago's South Side until the age of 13. The experience that I bring into this conversation, the anecdotal evidence that I will provide, and the lens that I view the world and this topic through is my own. It does not speak to or for every black woman, every mother of black boys,* and every child that grew up in the midst of crisis or experienced trauma. It is simply a glimpse into one person's perspective that is filled with nuance and the deep reflective work that led me right here, writing this message to you. My stories may be worlds away from your own, and I love that for you. You don't need to walk a mile in my shoes to arrive at the same destination. I state my truth in its totality without shame as it took the part of me that was fractured to become the me that stands whole before you now.

Because I am about to lay bare stories that have lived silently in my head and heart rent free—some for decades—I do not want to begin without giving an honor to them as my heart knows their names, but you do not. I hope you will take the time to honor them with me by saying their names before we begin.

Sammy, Terry, Daniel, Duke, Rob, Brian, Marcus, Tristan… We remember you always.

Teacher Toolkit

Let's open up our Teacher Toolkit. First tool we're adding in comes in the form of sage advice:

Don't follow me, I'm lost too.

1

Focusing on Self-Reflection

Self-reflection is one of the most important acts that we can do—as humans both in this world and in our work with young children. It is really a wonderful tool that we all have at our disposal—as long as we do the work to actually use it.

Throughout my years working with children, I have come to find the value and beauty of using self-reflection not only as a way to strengthen our practice with children but also as a way to strengthen ourselves, heal our inner child, and find peace within ourselves. So much of the work that we do with children each day can truly be work that we do on ourselves as well. By wanting to give children a safe and supportive space to come everyday, we also in turn are creating that for ourselves.

Now, self-reflection is not easy; like, at all. When we decide to do the work, we are deciding to possibly open up old wounds and things that we have not really dealt with or worked through. This can be difficult and bring up a lot of possibly unwanted emotions or feelings—but I promise you that if you commit to doing this work and commit to using self-reflection in your work, you will be better for it. A better adult and support for the children you work with and a better person for yourself!

I talk about self-reflection a lot when I am speaking with providers and educators because so much of our thoughts, our beliefs and our behaviors in our daily lives, and our work with children are informed by our lived experiences. I feel like we know this on a base level, right? But we don't truly understand it

DOI: 10.4324/9781032679808-2

or recognize it in our practice. And that is totally understandable! Our days are filled with so much! We are constantly on the go— both at work and at home. So it can be hard to focus on "hmmm, I wonder if the reason I said that has to do with something in my past." But don't worry, we are going to be focusing a lot on the practice of self-reflection in this book, and our goal is to help you think differently about your life, your practice with children, and your goals for your work with children.

Here are two ways that I share with people in regard to how to practice self-reflection in their practice with children:

> | *think about what it is that you want the children in your care to feel and experience when they are with you. What do you want them to gain from their time with you? When they leave you, what do you hope stays with them?*
>
> | *now, take that and write it down somewhere that you can see it on a daily basis-maybe a note on the mirror or something.*
>
> | *each day when you are thinking back and reflecting on the day, consider the things that happened, the things you did, and the things you said and think about whether those things align with the goals you wrote down on that note. If they do, great! Focus on cultivating that even more. If they do not, it is time for some deeper reflection.*
>
> | *think about what it is the children are doing that is making you uncomfortable or creating a desire in you to stop them*
>
> | *now, write this down and any emotions that come with it, and be honest with yourself. For example, "Seeing the chil- dren pretend to use guns makes me scared because I am afraid they will grow up to be harmful to others."*
>
> | *then, spend some time in reflection of your own childhood and lived experiences to see if you can make a connection between your feelings and your experiences.*
>
> | *refer back to the classroom agreements and truly think about the situation and if it is something that needs to be stopped or corrected.*

When we notice things that we do or say that may not align with what we strive to offer the children in our care, it is important for us to focus on those things and try to unpack where they come from and why we did them. This is the part that can be difficult. Let's say for instance that you raised your voice at the children on this day (who hasn't done that, right?). Now you come home and you feel guilty or upset at yourself for doing that. You recognize that is not in line with what you want the children to experience with you. So you start to unpack that experience. What was going on at the moment you raised your voice? What were the children doing? What made you upset? Maybe you felt like they were not listening to you—so why does that make you upset? Maybe you felt like the classroom was getting out of control—so what does out of control mean to you and why do you feel the need to keep everything in control? Start with those questions and think deeply about the answers and where those feelings come from. Then understand that raising your voice does not make you a bad teacher—what is important is that you do the work to understand why it happened and what you can do to deal with those feelings in a more productive way for the children.

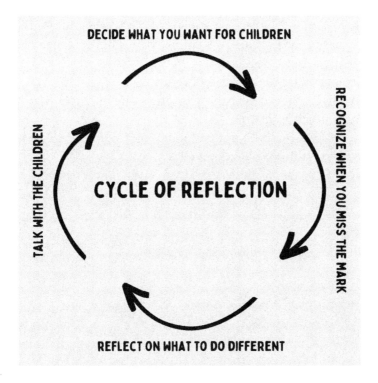

I wanted to explain a bit more in depth about this self-reflection process before we got into the ideas of this book because we will be using this idea of self-reflection many times throughout this book. It is what you get with me—lots of reflecting! Here is how that will look as you continue through this book:

| each chapter will have numerous opportunities for you to reflect not only on the chapter itself, but also on your own experiences and feelings. You will be able to do this directly into this book in the spaces provided.

| each chapter will also include prompt questions that you can use as you see fit to help you reflect on the reasons you do the things you do as a teacher.

| at the end of this book, there will be an opportunity for you to create an action plan for going forward in your work with children and will encourage you to think about how you will use what you have learned and discovered in this book right away with the children you work with.

Something important to remember about self-reflection: you have to be honest! Self-reflection is work that is just for you. If you cannot be honest in your reflections, you cannot expect to make any positive changes. So please, feel free to be completely honest in your responses to the reflection prompts, and I encourage you to only share these thoughts with others if YOU feel that it will be helpful to your journey.

So, are you ready? I am so excited and honored to be taking this journey with you. Let's dive in!

2

Making a Connection to Child Development

One of the things I took into consideration when coming up with the idea for this book was that many folx may say no to any form of weapon play because they do not feel or see it as being an important piece of a child's development. They are not able to see the positives or the pieces of this play that are developmentally informed and responsive. (This is a wonderful reframe in language for "developmentally appropriate" I heard from the wonderful Early Childhood Nerd Heather Bernt-Santy). Whether that is due to their own lived experiences, their own opinions, or something else. (We will get into that a bit deeper later in this book.)But it is important for us to recognize (no matter our personal feelings regarding this type of play) that this type of play *is* developmentally informed and responsive and is something that children are going to explore whether we discuss it with them in any way or not. Don't believe me? Think about it this way: did you explore any types of this play when you were a child? Did any of the children you knew or played with? I know for me, I was always playing good guys/bad guys, superheroes, and more. I have a feeling that you may be the same way. So if we know that, it is not a stretch to understand that this type of play is something that children are going to be interested or curious about more often than not.Also, there are SO many things that

DOI: 10.4324/9781032679808-3

HOW WEAPON PLAY CONNECTS TO CHILD DEVELOPMENT	
DEVELOPMENTAL DOMAIN	HOW IT CONNECTS
SOCIAL/EMOTIONAL	KINDNESS, CONSENT, EMPATHY
COGNITIVE	CRITICAL THINKING
LANGUAGE	SPEAKING FOR THEMSELVES, POWER
MATHEMATICS	SIZE, WEIGHT, HEIGHT, DIMENSIONS
FINE MOTOR	HANDLING SMALL OBJECTS
GROSS MOTOR	CLIMBING, JUMPING, SCALING

children can learn through this type of play. Let's take a look at some of the developmental milestones that we usually think about with young children and see how this type of play can connect to each of them.

As you can see, this type of play has many connections to a child's developmental milestones. This type of information can be a great tool to use when you are speaking to other adults about this type of play. It is also a great reminder for us, right? Sometimes, in our continued reflection and self-work, triggers may come up surrounding this play (even if we feel like we are on board with it completely!), and reminding ourselves of the benefits of this play can be very helpful.

It is also important for us to think about and consider the aspects of weapon play that connect to these milestones so that we can offer support and enhancement to the children's play. For instance, if we see children participating in this type of play, we can look at it, connect it to what they could learn from it, and encourage that learning:

"I see that you are using that stick as a weapon in your game, who are you in this game and how did you come up with that idea?" This is a simple question that we can ask to help solidify what it is the children are gaining from this type of play. This can also help the child to feel safe and secure in their play since more often than not, children understand that adults say no to this type of play so they may feel as if they need to hide it or pretend they aren't doing it. But when we engage with them during this play, we are showing them that it is ok and that we are supporting them in it. Again, this can also help support our own understanding of this play and our own journey with being more accepting of this play—as I always say conversations are so important.

What is also interesting to consider when we are thinking about this type of play and as we debate the developmental responsiveness of it is our own play when we were children. It is easy to assume that most of us engaged in this type of play when we were children, right? Either cowboys, or robbers, or cops, or superheroes. We talk a lot about self-reflection in this book, and that includes thinking about our own childhoods. Not only how they affect our ways of thinking as adults, but also the similarities in our childhoods and the childhoods of the children that we work with now.

Take a minute right now and think back to your own childhood—how did you play? Did you engage in this type of play at all? How was this type of play initiated? What did you enjoy about it? Then you can take this reflection and use it to inform you about the children you are working with currently.

Where can you see weapon play fitting into a child's development?

Sometimes, it can be helpful to go back into the mind of a child when we are working with children now.

Words from Kisa

I want to sit with Samuel's point about exploration for a beat. I grew up in a home where weapon play, with guns in particular, was a big no-no. And there was a good reason. To paint a portrait of my environment as a young girl on Chicago's South Side, we were a decade into the crack era, gang violence: drive-by shootings, bus checks, and carjackings, made hyper-vigilance the norm. Gangsta rap was still in its infancy, but it was cute, heavy-handed, and moving fast so you knew it was inevitable that it was going to do some damage. Though weapon play of any kind was forbidden in my home, my mom also happened to love Westerns, so old shows like *The Rifleman*, *Bonanza*, and *Gunsmoke* served as white noise in the background, while my twin sister and I played nearby. To be honest, even with the constant syndicated Westerns playing in the distance, we may have made it without breaking our home's cardinal rule if not for the release of 1990s blockbuster, *Young Guns II*. After that, it was, "I'll make you famous", surprise attacks with quick-draw pretend Revolver, all day, every day until my mother or grandmother heard us ...oh, the punishments we had. Did it make us stop? Absolutely not.

Conversely, the following year *Boyz n the Hood* hit the scene, and though my twin and I were riveted by the movie and could recite the words as we watched, it was not something that we reenacted in our play, not even surreptitiously. Though both movies depicted violence and included guns as the method of conducting said violence, one was suspended reality and the other was a reflection of the reality in which we lived. To imagine my twin and I as horse riding bandits, renegades, or outlaws was a fantastic image, and it was one we couldn't get enough of. To watch *Boyz n the Hood*, however, was like getting a sneak peek into the world we were being shielded from. The world that existed right outside our door, and it was cool on TV, but it was a world we wanted no part of, not even for pretend.

I don't know about you, Samuel, but this lens definitely plays a part in how I see weapon play within the learning space I share with children. I understand that though I wasn't able to articulate it, and I highly doubt that either myself or my twin understood it beyond our respective stages of development, we intuited that there was a huge difference between playing "cowboy" and playing "gangbanger," and I believe children, from any background, are capable of intuiting while they play. Just think about it: when children wrestle, they modify depending on the size of their opponent, feign injuries for entertainment, and even if they become dysregulated in the midst of their play, the intention is never malicious. The same goes for superhero play. A child can pretend to fly, have lasers for eyes, and a host of other super powers, but if you ask them to use said super powers to perform a task, they will instantly break character with confusion because they know that what they are pretending to do is not real and the request to make their suspended-disbelief selves do human things is jarring. Children shift between what is real and the fantastic seamlessly multiple times per day, and if this was a child pretending they were a firefighter, no, better yet a fire *engine*, no one in the room would bat an eye, but somehow when it comes to weapon play everyone rushes to do damage control to ensure that the child in our classroom isn't gearing up to be the biggest sociopath the world has ever seen. I have a few thoughts on why that might be. So let's get into it.

The baggage that we bring into our classrooms comes in the form of our worldview, and if our goal is getting to the root of the problem, then the best practice is gonna be to decrease the load created by the beliefs, values, expectations, and stories *we* carry into every environment we enter.

Here is the part where things get a bit dicey. In order for us to disentangle our worldview from the image of the child, we have to first familiarize ourselves with the discomfort of being self-reflective and the sting of doing self-work. It would be great to assume that everyone reading these pages has an understanding of what is required of them, but I think it is vital to approach this particular segment from the perspective of the novice so that everyone, reflective practitioner and those looking to establish a reflective practice alike, can walk away with tools they can incorporate into their learning spaces.

Many of you may not know me and are coming to know me through my writing, so I think it's important for you to know the style in which I present things. There are going to be many books that market a particular method as a solution to whatever educational pain points you may have. And while I am not challenging the efficacy of that method, I do not share this approach. I know what I know and that's all that I know, and that does not include the answers that you may seek. *My way* is to set the stage that will pique your curiosity, and on that stage, we all have roles. My role is to ask the right questions that will inspire you to dig deeper and dismantle the parts within that aren't serving you or the children that you share space with. Your job is to wonder what you're doing, why you're doing it, and who it serves. Together our role will be to reimagine all the possibilities for our children when we know better and act upon that knowledge in order to have a practice that is both developmentally responsive and informed. Get it? Got it? Good. Let's unpack, shall we?

For quite some time, there has been a single story painted about weapon play, and it is one that has been painted with a broad brush. That story is one of gender, violence, and aggression. *"Boys* will be boys" is heard as *boys will be violent and aggressive*. A child carrying a stick is typically seen as having ill intent—they will hurt someone and that act of aggression is sure to be intentional. Gunplay, rock play, good guy vs. bad guy play are violent, dangerous, and threatening, and on the story goes. Everything I just wrote has been heard before: in learning spaces, public spaces, and the privacy of your own homes. The issue with them is twofold, really. The first issue is that the story is based on binary thinking. Binary thinking happens when nuanced ideas, concepts, behaviors, and problems are simplified into an either/ or perspective. The child that is exhibiting rough-and-tumble play can *only* be aggressive. The child throwing the rocks at no one and nothing in particular can *only* be destructive. The child infusing weapons into their imaginative play can *only* be violent. This mindset creates the unwritten rules which govern our learning environments and results in the framework of our culture being guided by a single perspective: your own. This is pedagogical risky business as the line between guiding and modeling behaviors becomes blended with personal assumptions, beliefs, and the values we attribute to them. I want to expound on this idea for a bit so that my educators can really think about why our binary thinking may be problematic and I am going to use the example of swordplay.

In many learning environments, swordplay is perfectly acceptable, and it's not out of place to see a foam sword in an easily accessible area of the dress-up section. In many Waldorf inspired environments, it is even celebrated. The children sand, stain, and paint their swords. Learn songs about a magical blade that defeats a dragon and saves the people of the land. It's a beautiful story, really, and a cool way to create a meaningful experience with children. My question is, have you ever seen what a sword can do? We're talking: hacking, slashing, impaling…beheading. But that is not the narrative for this particular story. The narrative here is that the sword is noble; it is dignified, skillful, even. Let's think about gun play on the other hand. You will never find a pretend gun anywhere in any public early learning environments; there will be no songs made about the gun-slinging hero that single-handedly took out the bad guys and saved the people of the land, and there surely won't be any collaborative projects between caregiver and child that involves the crafting of a firearm. No way. I'm going to take the liberty of using words that I plucked straight from an online blog that described contrasting views of gun and swordplay, and in it the author used the words, "awful, undignified, thuggish and unpleasant." What is the difference between the two? Both could be used to cause harm to self and others if found by a child in real life, or misused and abused by someone older. Both have been historically used to commit acts of violence and used in aggression. If we're trying to veer our children away from the pretense of bloodshed by choosing swordplay over gunplay, then we're going in the wrong direction. My theory is that the only difference between the two is the person who is spinning the tale about their value.

According to the 2023 demographics and statistics, the racial distribution at Waldorf schools is over 50% white, nearly 20% Latino, 10% Asian, and 8% black.

You see where I'm going here? *Good*, because it'll lead us right into the second issue.

The narrator of our storylines is the keeper of the power. Some of our most entrenched beliefs of racism, classism, sexism, ableism, etc., were created through systems and structures we weren't present for. Nevertheless, we all carry them subconsciously. They are ancestral, generational, and communal. Being cognizant of this fact allows us to reclaim agency of thought, and changing your thoughts will be the hardest part of the battle.

Before we move into unpacking our mindset, I want to unzip this tiny bag pushed off to the side that packs a mighty punch. In it, you will find a couple of stand-alone concepts that negatively impact the narrator and require deeper consideration before we go spinning our tales, and that is control and unreasonable expectations. The two work in tandem, especially in an early learning environment, and if left unchecked can introduce our young geniuses through a prickly conduit to the preschool to prison nexus.

Unreasonable Expectations

Okay, I think Samuel already established the pages of this book as a judgment free space, and I'm grateful for it, 'cause it's confession time. Something that could throw my often composed, knowledgeable, over four decades old self into a tizzy in 2.3 seconds was a child pointing anything: a stick, a block, a tinker toy, or their finger in my direction and firing. For whatever reason, my natural response to such behavior was to throw my hands up, turn away, and recoil...from nothing. I have raised my voice because of it, I have confiscated the preferred weapon of choice (except the fingers, of course), and, shamefully, I have given timeouts over it because, well, you shot your teacher in the face. *How dare you?* In retrospect, the only person that deserved a timeout for this nonsensical behavior was the adult giving a child a consequence over something they did in their imagination.

This is akin to reprimanding a child for burning me with the tea at an imaginary tea party. *Who does that?*

An adult's ability to place value and intention on the acts of a child who has an entirely different set of rules for processing information and behavior is uncanny at best, cruel and unusual at its worst. A child works on cause and effect. *I do this, and that happens as a result.* So the value is in seeing what will happen if I do ___? The intention is to see what will happen once I do ____? And they will keep repeating the same behavior until they have learned what the desired result is. It is just that simple—no malicious intent, no bad behavior, just a child meaning-making through dramatic play.

If a "Karen" was a construct, she would show up in the form of control. The feeling that classrooms need management, rules, consequences, incentives, quiet, obedience, and a hierarchical structure is all based on a need to control the environment the children that we serve move around in. There is a responsibility we have as practitioners to control aspects of the environment in order to nurture the genius within our children, but I'm not talking about that. I'm talking about controlling the environment by way of controlling the child. We eliminate everything that resembles a weapon, snatch up every rock in our field, and toss away every fallen branch in order to control the outcome. We *think* this is a proactive approach and that the children are only tempted to behave aggressively when they are incited by items that encourage aggressive behavior. The problem with this theory is the more we strive for control, the more resourceful our little friends become. They find clever ways to create their own weapons in their secret makerspace. They develop a coded language for weapons, shooting, and power wielding in their play. Does this make our clever geniuses sneaky, disrespectful, or disobedient? Actually, no. In fact, I'd argue that this work-around was a healthy display of their budding agency and the innate need all human beings have to be autonomous. Rather than viewing this behavior as a breach of the rules, I challenge you to view it as behavioral communication. Lucky for you, I happen to speak fluent child behavior so I can translate. The behavior says: *You're doing too much, teach.* Loosen the reins a lil bit.

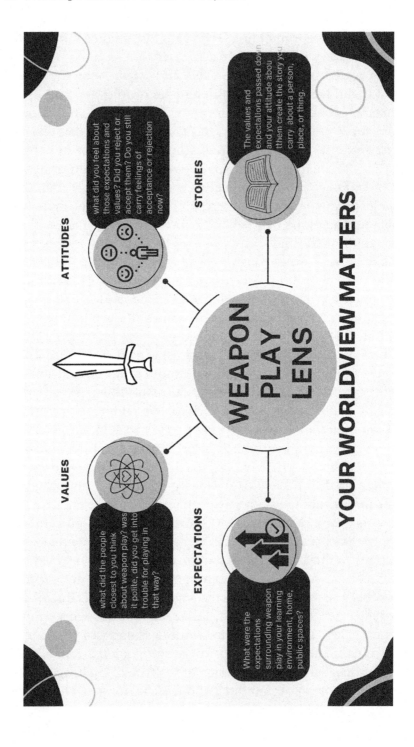

Alright, now that we've distinguished between reasonable and unreasonable expectations, and relinquished control, we now have the capacity to take on a little bit (heard as a hell of a lot) of self-work! This is the heaviest part of the bag we're unloading so it may be a little uncomfortable, but remember, unpacking your worldview is not indicative of a *you* problem. The complexities of our worldview are universal. Our lived experiences are unique to our culture and communities; to our personal lives, and within our family structure. It is what makes us the wonderful caregivers and educators that we are. The only problem is when we are not aware of how our lived experiences show up—and they will show up—through a child's behavior, wants, needs, and the things that they say and do. If we are not aware, this can cause blindspots in our practice because we are being activated and become reactive instead of responding in a developmentally informed way. This is why knowing our worldview matters.

Let's *pause f*or a minute. Throughout my segments, you will come across breaks in the text when I prompt you to reflect. If you see, *"full stop"*, I'm prompting you to feel whatever it is the text conjures up for you. If you come across a full stop prompt and you don't feel any physical response in your body, disregard and continue reading. Let's continue.

Again, with the assumption that you are a complete novice, I want to go over a few terms before we jump into the questions in this exercise to ensure that we all have a clear understanding. Using the chart as our visual reminder, we're going to break down our worldview with scenarios depicting how each would show up in an early learning setting.

Values: Values are the moral and ethical guidelines that govern how individuals navigate social groups and evaluate themselves and the environment in which they live. Values inform our thoughts, actions, and beliefs, and dictate what is a priority and what is inconsequential.

In an early learning environment, our strong values against weapon play would express itself in a teacher observing children playing with bristle blocks, noticing that one of them has created a gun by interlocking two of the blocks, interrupting the play by removing the pink and green beretta from the toddler's hands while insisting, "We don't do that here!" *That*, meaning gunplay, is valued as wrong, bad, inappropriate so the natural response is to ensure that the play ceases immediately.

Our values would also lead a more reflective teacher who understood that she shouldn't interrupt the child's play, and being cognizant of the fact that the child had a desire for power, going into the dress-up bin and handing them a sword in exchange for the beretta. This teacher may be perfectly well intentioned, but it is her values that made her think that a sword that is used for violence has a higher value than a gun that is used for violence, and that is problematic.

Expectations: Expectations are the directives set forth based upon your personal value system or the value structure of your social group. In short, your expectations are the unwritten rules that organize and manage your life and learning environment.

Using the same example from above, the expectation is that "we," meaning, the entire classroom, will not participate in weapon play. But to broaden our understanding it is also expressed when we are out on a nature walk and reprimand a child for picking up a stick or a rock. The expectation is that the children will look at those natural items with their eyes and refrain from picking them up.

Attitudes: Attitudes reflect our thoughts, feelings, and dispositions, and the manner in which we approach or respond to a situation. An educator's disposition or attitude determines the culture of your learning environment. Think back to the power of the person spinning the tale: *Are we the Lion or the Hunter?* Using the worldview graphic above, our attitudes towards weapon play would be to assign judgment on the play and/or the person participating in the play. The guns are *violent*, and the child's expression of violence will negatively impact the culture of the classroom. I've seen this go as far as an educator attributing the "violent" behavior to unknown and unfounded domestic abuse or other forms of unseen yet assumed family dysfunction.

Stories

The values, expectations, and attitudes that we possess make up the stories that we tell ourselves about our self-image, the image we have for the children in our learning environment, their families, and the culture at large. Our stories are largely linked to our attitudes as they measure how we feel about a particular person, place, or thing, and they communicate our disposition about a subject through the way that we interact in relationship with others.

I want to come back around to the danger of a single story. A single story is that let's give the child a name, Timothy, who created the bristle block beretta in the corner of the block area is violent because his father is violent. The single story is based off of the few transactions a caregiver had with Timmy's father when he wasn't openly affectionate with Timothy at drop-off. Through the caregiver's lens, he stood over the child in an intimidating way, his voice was gruff, and he was not affable enough for her liking. This story makes no room for nuances like fatigue, whether the father was or was not a morning person or having a natural gravelly timbre. It also doesn't make space for racial and cultural differences. Timothy's dad may have looked intimidating to her because his six foot, five inch frame overshadowed her by a foot and a half. But that wouldn't necessarily be intimidating to Timothy who only knows that very tall man as his father. I could take us deeper down this rabbit hole, but I won't. The bottom line is that our judgments are based on our ideas of a person, place, or thing, and those judgments are an expression of our biases, and if our implicit biases are running the show, then many of our children are in trouble.

Question time! If our biases are implicit, how do we know when they are running the show? In the midst of an exchange where you have placed value or judgment on a child or their grownup caregiver, ask yourselves, "Is this the way that I *feel* about the situation or do I know this to be true?"

In my interpersonal relationships with adults, I try to keep in mind that my feelings are helpful and valid, but they are often intangible and subjective. The facts, on the other hand, the facts are always real and true.

What is real and true about this hypothetical situation of a boy, his beretta, and his Baba? None of it, 'cause it's hypothetical. But I'm using it to illustrate how grown-up caregivers get our feelings entangled with the facts and that is part and parcel of the problem with weapon play.

The truth is, I cannot say that there haven't been times when weapon play has not resulted from a violent or aggressive act that a child may have witnessed and later emulated in their learning environment. What I am saying is those instances are largely the exception and not the rule. And if it is not the rule, then we need to make space for considering why it is that we feel the way that we feel about this particular form of play, and in order to do that we will need to look closely at our own lens. That said, let's get into our questions.

1. What messages did you receive about weapon play as a child?
2. Whose worldview did it center?
3. Which unwritten rules about weapon play have you brought into your learning environment?
4. Who or what is spinning the tale?
5. Who is the narrator?

Teacher Toolkit

Reflections!

Feelings are sometimes helpful and always valid,
Facts are invariably real and true.

3

Defining Weapon Play

Ok, time to dive into what we are talking about in this book. We've prepared ourselves by discussing the importance of self-reflection as well as discussing what our goal is for this book: not to convince you to celebrate and encourage weapon play, but to help you to think differently and deeper about weapon play and your practice as a whole.

When we are talking about weapon play, it is important to make sure that we understand what type of play we are talking about and what it may look like in a childcare program. Weapon play can take on many different forms and look very different from program to program and from child to child. When children are engaging in weapon play, they could be:

| using sticks as swords, guns, or knifes| using rocks as "bombs"| using toy guns or weapons| using their hands as weapons| using their words as weapons| pretending to be the "bad guy" or the "good guy"| acting out scenes from TV or movies| playing "war"| "blowing" things up| creating armies| and many more…| can you think of any more ways that children may be engaging in this type of play that you have seen?

This is where it can get a little uncomfortable for us, right? We see these examples of play, and we think-"oh this sounds horrible! I don't think the children should be doing this!" That is

DOI: 10.4324/9781032679808-4

why it was important for us to first focus on what the children can gain in terms of their development through this play. (And why it is important for us to remember those things as we continue on in this journey.)

I think now it would be a good time to stop and reflect. I want you to take a few minutes to sit with the feelings that you have as you read through the types of weapon play in the list above. I want you to be able to name and recognize those feelings first. Then, I want you to reflect on where those feelings come from, why you have them, and what you think they mean. Finally, I want you to consider if there are ways that you can work through those feelings (if they are suggesting to you that this type of play is not acceptable) to think about this play in a different way. This was something that I had to do in a big way when I started to shift my thinking around weapon play, because I was the teacher who was against it in all forms for many years.

Words from Kisa

I wholeheartedly agree with you, Samuel. An introduction to weapon play in any setting should come with a trigger warning because it activates so many, especially in American culture.

Due to its inherent complexities, it is a trickier one to incorporate throughout all learning spaces. However, it is no less vital to a child's development. Again, weapon play can look like children using sticks as swords, lego "pewers," as my crew calls them, or having imaginative duels that end when someone is "deaded."

This play conjures societal issues like mass shootings, police brutality, and street violence, and makes adults cringe and even intervene when they see it, but those societal issues are adult problems that have nothing to do with child's play.

I distinctly recall two of my crew playing one day and one of them instructing the other, "okay, shoot me and I'm dead." I already had my camera going for documentation of their play, and it captured the whole scenario in real time: one child uses a finger gun, points, and shoots. The other falls dramatically to the ground and lays out flat after being felled by an imaginary bullet.

My intention at the end of the night was to write a piece on the importance of weapon play, but I never made it to that point because the sight of the felled and pretend lifeless child on our playroom floor, who also happened to be black and assigned male at birth, was so upsetting that I wound up deleting the footage. Just the thought of watching it made me feel physically ill and deleting the entire affair was the only thing that brought me back to a space where I could get out of my own head and show up fully for the children who were in front of me.

Now, my quiet observers know that all footage is fodder for learning—even the kind that makes our hearts sting. However, my personal history caused me to interpret this imaginative experience through a lens of gun violence, race, and familial trauma. And while I didn't interrupt the play, I did erase the experience which in hindsight may have been even worse had I not figured out that I could relay the message without footage, help myself, and hopefully teach others in the process. My experiences as a human being matter and showed up live and in living color that afternoon. As caregivers our human experiences will inevitably color the way that we see situations in our learning environments, and for that we will need to call a thing a thing and give ourselves grace. In my case, the gun—finger made or otherwise—the death, and black body on the ground served as a trigger inciting decades of hurt and violence, and I no longer saw child's play, only the impact that this hurt and violence had on black and brown bodies—male-assigned bodies in particular.

Okay…I need to take a breath after that one, because I'm human and in my humanity this issue is one that activates me even when recalled for the purpose of learning.

Alongside of my very real emotions and experiences is the fact that this type of play isn't about violence, malice, or injustice. Weapon play and its cannon toting cousin power play are about efficacy, bravery, heroism, and empowerment, and children, even those who live in high crime areas like I did, are playing out scenarios just like they do in all the other forms of play, to make it make sense to them.

Children are not playing with weapons as an act of aggression or violence, or to idolize the offender. The weapons—whether imagined, illustrated, foam, nature provided, or formed with their body—represent power and children are wielding that power to imagine a world where they, tiny but mighty as they are, are the first line of defense. Let's imagine this scenario if we were curious before assigning intent. If we took a second before reacting to the behavior and asked ourselves, *Is it helpful*? Is restricting whatever display of weapon play the children are exhibiting responsive to their age and stage of development? *Is it necessary*? Is harm being done to people or property which requires you to intervene? *Is it kind?* Is prohibiting weapon play informed by what you know about child development or informed by your worldview? Yes, we understand that we live in a world wrought with social injustice, mass shootings, and gun violence, but we also know that a child is not yet capable of understanding everything that goes into gun control, gun reform, institutionalized racism, the inadequacies in the mental healthcare system, and the root conditions leading to street violence, and the expectation that they would be is an unreasonable one. What they are capable of perceiving is fear, and since children are concrete thinkers, telling them that they are safe checks the kindness box, but there is room for what is helpful and necessary, and they can sort that all out through their play. They won't sort it out in the way that we would as adults. They sort it out in a way that is both responsive to their development and informed by it. Let's sit with how impactful this adult reframe could be in the lives of the children that we serve.

So even if it isn't permitted in a daycare center or on the school playground, we as educators should at least change our mindsets as to why it is being done.

Teacher Toolkit

Reflections!

Ask yourself:
    Is it helpful?
    Is it necessary?
    Is it kind?
    Weapon play goes as far back as the children of cavemen, but on record, gunplay runs alongside war. Older than the electric streetcar, the lightbulb, the airplane, the hamburger, automobile, and coca-cola are toy guns. For over 150 years children have been using guns in their play, but it was by chance that a business offering farmers a metal version of an air rifle for free with a purchase of their windmill, that production really took off. In less than five years, the company had distributed over 50,000 rifles—not across the country—within 100 miles! What does any of this mean? That historically children used weapon play to create meaning-making for over a millennia before they were taboo. Did adult-centered desires lead to the creation of toy guns? It's likely. Did they create weapon play? Highly unlikely. The other thing that history tells us that children create the rules, roles, and complexities of their play and don't suffer much input

Timeline of Weapon Play

1930's
The Great Depression

Buck Rogers Pocket Pistol
WWI Naval Aviator
The First BB gun

1940's
War Games

plastic army men, submarine & torpedo, bombing games & Real guns

1950's
Strategy Implementation

cap guns, caps, bow and arrow, plastic bowie knife, rifles, sticks and rocks, ray guns, plastic grenades & war toys

1960's
war toy spike

toy pistol, space gun and flash light, Guerrilla Warfare Set, G.I. Joe, and that really problematic Cowboy Game

1970's
Knowledge Transfer

battleship, clackers, lawn darts, cowboy

1980's
Data Collection and Analysis

Star Wars, He Man, Wrestling Figures, water guns, clackers, Dungeons & Dragons Figure, Teenage Mutant Ninja Turtles

1990's
Solution Development

Supersoaker, Power Rangers, Pretend Wrestling, Cops & Robbers, Nerf guns

2000's
Video Game Era

Bubble gun, Marvel Hammer, Ninja toys, Transformers Merchandise, imaginary play (soldier, police officer, sheriff, etc.)

2010's
Decline of Outdoor Play

shield & sword, axe, and dagger

2020's
Relationship Management

majority of weapon play is imaginary, including superhero play, stick & rock play, and tag.

from adults when it comes to imaginative design. And there will be no unwarranted architectural assistants in their game.

If history documents weapon play back 150 years, when did it become improper in public spaces and inadmissible in learning environments? Answering this question has proven difficult. Information pertaining to the ban on weapon play specifically has proven to be elusive. What is clear to see is the uptick in school shootings from the Columbine Massacre of 1999 until the present. It's reasonable to think that school officials began to correlate school violence to "violent" play and banned it in an effort to keep everyone safe. The issue here is that if there were no real weapons and young children were simply pretending, what would the children be kept safe from, exactly?

It can't be denied that from 1840 to 1999 there were 300 recorded school shootings, and in the 23 years since Columbine, there have been 389. As Jay-Z once infamously said after snagging his award at the MTV awards, *Men* lie, Women* lie, numbers don't.*

If the argument was about gun free zones, or gun safety reform, then you would hear no argument from me. But that's not how weapon play works. It's not how any of it works at all. There shouldn't be a line item in the code of conduct for young children that includes the creation of a gun with your hands. There should be no disciplinary action for young children for saying things like, "I'm going to shoot you," during their play… Let me be specific here because I don't want people to miss the message. I am not speaking about a child who actually threatens violence, which may be indicative of a larger problem and require intervention from a school counselor or another trained professional. I am speaking about children playing an innocent imaginative game, and one of the two players says, "I'm gonna shoot you!" We have to think long and hard about why we are jumping the figurative gun, pun intended, and assigning violent intent to a young child's play, and chances are it all leads back to the views of the adults and not actions of the child.

Coloring Weapon Play

Samuel, we'd be remiss to have a conversation on this topic without talking about weapon play's "black tax." For those of you who are unaware of the term, black tax refers to the toll racial inequities place on the standard of living, and it is all encompassing—from actual finances and living wage, education, career, etc. And it begins where? You guessed it, early childhood.

I think about the disproportionate number of Global Majority children suspended, expelled, or walked out in handcuffs due to zero tolerance policies. I think about how the innocence of youth is cut short by years when black children, especially black boys, cease being cute and start becoming a threat under the gaze of implicit bias. I think about children like Nicholas Heyward Jr., Tamir Rice, and Andy Lopez who didn't have the luxury of weapon play afforded to so many of their white peers, and I wonder if black and brown children can afford another fatal double standard to add to a load that is already too heavy for our children to bear.

This is where we stumble upon the weapon toting elephant in the room and its presence cannot be denied; even for the purpose of this book as again, we are not creating revisionist history. We understand the nation in which we live and how issues of systemic racism infiltrate every facet of our lives, right down to the way in which our children play.

So where does that leave our black, brown, differently abled, and queer children? Do we resolve that they are exempt from the benefits of play designed to make meaning of the world because there is even less room for their humanity than the fraction that is allotted to children in the first place? Absolutely not. We disrupt dehumanization. We interrupt the narrative that there is one way for BIPOC, neurodivergent, and neurodiverse children to exist and another for white atypical children. We advocate, we inform, we start to have uncomfortable conversations, and we let the children play.

Play Techniques with Kisa

The play techniques that I will be describing are considered to be "renegade" by some, and that's precisely why there should be space for them in your early learning environment. To be clear, educators don't need access to a field to wrestle on, a lumber or a forest preserve to round up sticks, or a pretend arsenal for them to get their Global Integrated Joint Operating Entity (GI Jo(e)) on. The only thing required in your learning environment is consideration that any of these techniques has cognitive benefits, which they do.

> *First rule: Let go of everything you thought about rough & tumble play*
> *Second rule: reimagine rough & tumble play*

I was en route to my favorite neighborhood bookstore the other day when I heard a commotion across the street. There were two people with the unmistakable markers of a heated debate: One rose from their seat quickly, voice elevated, their intonation hitting every point; the other, head turning in disagreement as if whacking every syllable back to their opponent, infuriated palms slapping together as they shouted their position in their challenger's direction. I thought two things as I observed onlookers stopping what they were doing to view, and even record the exchange:

1. This is none of my business.
2. Let me get the hell out of dodge.

This is the exact feeling I imagine many non-care working adults have when they see children fighting over, let's say, a ball. I even had a parent tell me that watching the kids passionately negotiate over whose turn it was to get on a swing, *stressed them out*, before making a beeline for the door.

Rough-and-tumble play, like other forms of risky play, make grown-ups uncomfortable. But there's no need for alarm. Unlike the melee that went down near the bookstore, there will be no police intervention required to break up this fight; in fact, there is no need for any intervention at all! A couple of years ago I started a mantra about my obligations as a provider, and it's a simple one that you should take a moment to add to your toolkit.

Teacher Toolkit

Reflections!

If you aren't making space for play, you're in the way.

Rough-and-tumble play was probably the last mental road-block I had to unlock, and understandably so! *Why would children want to hurt each other, and, more importantly, why would any adult in a childcare capacity allow it? What if someone gets injured? What will the stakeholders think? What about licensing?* The uncertainty about the answers to this flurry of questions usually results in the same old script heard in early learning spaces across the country, and maybe even beyond:

"We don't do ___ here!" You can insert any rough-and-tumble behavior here, and then I'm going to fill you in on a little known fact:

They did
& they do
& they will

Because it is innate. Through creating rules, negotiating when things aren't going as planned, as well as trial and error, they are learning consent, limitations, and what their capabilities are, and they are tapping into the one thing that consumes the minds of all little people: power.

So, I got out of the way and took them to a field to play in their way!

How would this look in various learning spaces? Well, because of the constant threat of litigation, we understand that many forms of rough-and-tumble play are prohibited, so I will do my best to illustrate what rough-and-tumble play looks like in the spaces where they can be permitted as well as what we as educators can consider about why it is being done and the way that we feel about it.

Painting Rough-and-Tumble Play

During quarantine parents with toddlers near and far were purchasing the modular foam couches for their little ones to get their big body play on, but who are we kidding? Every family can't afford to dole out $200 on what amounts to a really cool pillow forte, and neither can every provider. The equitable approach would be to devote space in the house for rough-and-tumble play with mats, cushions, or something soft to break their fall. If there isn't enough space to accommodate this type of play inside and you have access to grassy space outside or a nearby park, you can take advantage of that. One year, I had five children that were into rough-and-tumble play. My house is not huge, and it definitely wasn't big enough to hold five sets of rumbling, rolling legs, arms, and bodies. Our place for childhood is about four blocks down from a neighborhood park and small soccer field so we dubbed it our "fight field" and headed over there several times a week to get out our energy in a very big way.

For our differently abled companions, rough-and-tumble play could look like a tickle war, a chase, a piggyback ride, or growling like animals.

Stick Play

While rough-and-tumble play was hardest for me to make space for, I know countless providers who struggle with making space for stick play. The fear of a child poking their eye or the eye of another, scratching themself or another, or impaling themselves *or another*. Is enough to send a provider into a tizzy when a child looks in a twig's direction during a nature walk!

Stick play includes using sticks as swords, digging holes with sticks, or excavating dirt with sticks. Children can turn sticks into imaginative weapons and use them for battle. They can use sticks as writing tools, magic wands, flatware, canes, and so much more. Plus, stick play checks nearly every play for all boxes and only needs to be slightly modified if your companion has a limb difference.

Painting Stick Play

Painting stick play looks like seeing that stick as real and true. What size is it? How pokey is it? If you are concerned with the child holding the stick getting hurt, can you guide them through

36 ◆ Defining Weapon Play

a few tips that will help keep them safe? If you are worried that your stick wielding companion will hurt someone else, is there a way that you can tell them what the child they are too close to could be thinking if they are too young to say it themselves? This would sound like, "Hazel, I see Phoenix's eyes a little bunched up and she's looking at that stick as it gets closer to her belly. I'm not sure if she wants that. Phoenix, do you want that stick to touch you? If a child is old enough for emergent self-advocacy, you can repeat what the child says to ensure that the stick holder processed the information. This sounds like (child screams out, then you repeat.), and you say, "Jackson, I heard Logan say you scratched him. Is there a way you can hold the stick safely?"

War Play

The concept of war play is a bit different, and I would consider it a distinct form of play based on children who have a military frame of reference. There are still programs like Star Wars, Black Panther, and Avengers with soldiers and war themes, but by and large they are viewed by a crowd beyond the early years. Still, if a child has older siblings or has been exposed to these themes, they will inevitably be intrigued and want to share it with their friends so they can explore it further, and you know what? That should be okay.

Painting war play can look like children pretending to be soldiers either inside or outdoors. It can involve one child darting through the room and playing imaginatively on their own, or include one child hiding in wait for their classmates and jumping out for the element of surprise. It can get loud, and it may even look a bit chaotic depending on how many soldiers have joined in, but you can use your observational skills and your experience with the children in your care to gauge if it is something that the children can manage or if you need to guide them in creating your environment's war rules.

The bottom line is that children need conflict to stretch their emerging problem-solving skills, and this is not limited to physicality; this includes verbal sparring as well as social-emotional risky play, and the play we do in our minds when safety is an issue. The work is in seeing what is real and true in this behavior. Our children are not looking to do harm, they are exerting power, exploring empathy, cause and effect and they are tackling heavy issues in the only way that they know how.

Teaching with Trauma: A Cautionary Tale

Picture it: it's nearly noon on a slow moving afternoon in a home-based daycare. I am putting the finishing touches on lunch as the children play in various places around me. Some are across the room building an animal trap out of magna tiles, a few are nestled in on the couch "eye buying" every item in a retail magazine's holiday catalog, and on this particular day, two of my companions are sitting at the island across from me. The day is as uneventful as it gets, the speaker sets the vibe with a little jazz R&B, and my mind is on everything and nothing at all when I hear, "You wanna see it?" My Spidey senses start to tingle. I give a little glance over my shoulder as I place the lid back over the pasta that is cooking and see one child placing his hand over a stick being pointed in his direction. The child that is grasping the stick is visibly enjoying the exchange. He is smiling and playfully turning away, and the words, "No, you're gonna shoot me!" come out in between giggles.

My ears get hot, my heartbeat accelerates. I'm pausing, I'm pausing. Breathe.

The child pointing the stick at his friend squeals with delight. "It's too late, you're dead!" The game leads to a chase. "We're going outside, Ms. Kisa!" Through gritted teeth, I force out our community agreements, "Be safe, be kind, have fun!" I turn back to my food. All of my senses are heightened. The music is too loud, the room is too warm, and my stomach feels queasy. The children have gone on about their business, blissfully unaware that their play has just taken me back in time to a place where I didn't want to be.

I don't think we should talk about Daniel no more.

Trigger Warning: Accidental Shooting

In middle school, my twin sister, Danielle, was a member of a junior bowling league. Every Saturday, my mom and I would take her to the bowling alley in our neighborhood where she would meet up with her league of buddies, including our neighbor,

Salem, who lived directly across the street. Danie made great friends at the league. They traveled to different tournaments together, hung out, and invited one another to parties. Since I wasn't a part of the league, I didn't know anyone well, but I did get to attend a house party Danie got invited to once. There I met and danced with a boy named Daniel. He wasn't the boy next door cute. He had the preteen appeal of a character on television: he was tall for the age that we were, with golden brown skin, big eyes, and a nice smile—a lot like Stanley, Rudy Huxtable's boyfriend on the Cosby Show. The dance was awkward and slow, but he was polite and kind, and when it was over, I was relieved, but I also felt like for the first time in that dark room filled with strangers; I knew someone other than the person I shared a womb with. After the party ended, days went by like they do in your youth: slowly. Afternoons, weekends, and seasons all look the same in my mind's eye. I do know that we were in middle school and party lines were super popular. Danie was always on a party line with her bowling friends. One day, a day like all the rest before them, Danie chatted on the party line while I sat on the floor and drew pictures of whatever made up drama filled my head. That day she wasn't on the phone long. She got off the phone and went on to something else and that night everything changed. The phone rang and Danie cried on the floor. "We were just talking to him," she told my mother through sobs. Who? She talked to so many people and my heart raced as I tried to guess who she was speaking about. It was Daniel, her bowling mate. The cute boy I'd danced with at the party. The one that had been kind even though the song went on for too long. He'd been on the party line with Danie and my neighbor Salem. According to Danie, they hadn't been on the call for ten minutes when Daniel unexpectedly cut the call short. He told them that his neighbor had come over and he was about to go over to his house. Salem, who must have known more than everyone else, said, "Don't you do that." and Daniel promised that he wouldn't. And now we all knew what that thing was. The neighbor had found his father's gun, and together, they had been planning to check it out. They didn't know it was loaded or how to use it, and within moments, Daniel was gone. For weeks the league mourned the loss of their close friend. For months Daniel's mother came to the bowling alley every Saturday and sat in his seat. Sometimes she just sat there, sometimes she walked around like a zombie, other times she cried. The founder of the Bowling League asked her to stop coming after she brought Daniel's morgue photos to show everyone what would happen if they played with guns. One day, Salem told Danie, "I don't think we should talk about Daniel no more." and we never did.

Thirty years since I had thought about that night. Thirty years since I'd talked about what happened or connected the name Daniel with the face of the boy who we no longer spoke about. And suddenly, this play had brought up a wave of instances that were so heavy, and my mind wanted me to forget that they even happened. That's the tricky thing about triggers; they're sure to pop out when trauma or issues leading up to the trauma haven't been addressed.

Some of you may be thinking, that sounds like torture. What gifts does she receive from this interaction? Why wouldn't you just ban the children from weapon play? And my answer is the same as it has been through this long and arduous road, and that is to continue the work. Often, in the field of working with children, we assume the position that we are here to fix the broken things in the little people that we serve. We are educating them, andwe are seeing, hearing, and affirming them. If they have been harmed, then the goal is for our love to be the balm that protects them through their healing. But who heals the healer? The part of the work that we don't talk about enough is the self-work necessary to show up and do no harm in our field. We can't guide a child's learning in a way that aligns with their needs and stage of development if we as educators don't have a comprehensive understanding of what those individual needs are. We can desire it, we can even perform, but we cannot appreciate the value in a child being seen, heard, and respected until we know how empowering visibility, having a voice, and being affirmed is… we cannot be trauma informed when our traumas, past and/or present, are lying in wait like the child playing war games earlier in the book.

Full Stop

We cannot heal what we cannot heal.

Know thyself. Love thyself. Heal thyself. This is a massive undertaking, I get it. One of the things that first made me vibe with Samuel is our shared commitment to healing our inner child. When we are talking about reflective work, intentional work, and restorative work, we have to include self as a part of *the work*. There is so much that goes into self work, and that may include but isn't limited to a higher wage, the ability to utilize mental health days, and accessibility to mental wellness care.

It took a long time until I had access to any of those things, so trust me, I really do get it. But just as this book is a plea to rethink the way that we view weapon play, the caveat is that it will start with rethinking about yourself. Once we cross that hurdle, we will be able to view the way that we care for our children through a new lens—one that knows our hurts, hears our whispers, sees who we are at the core, and still says, you belong here too.

Teacher Toolkit

Reflections!

Ask yourself:

Is it real and true?

Or *your worldview*?

That one time, when my cat got murdered, and other types of death play…

Samuel, my friend, I know you and Perry are very much dog people. I see you with your boys, and I can only imagine that they are spoiled rotten to their furry little cores. But I'm a cat girl through and through, and I don't remember being anything else. I have had cats all of my life, and when I didn't have them, I obsessed over what life would be like when I reunited with them once more, so as you can imagine, nothing brought me more joy than that June in 2016 when we moved into a space and could have cats once more.

Along with my eldest son, we drove to the far side of the moon to get two five-week-old kittens who we named K-Ci and Jo-Jo. Well, we named them Daenerys and Stokley Carmichael, but our mother of dragons turned out to be a father, and Stockley was Cuckoo-Bananas and definitely didn't give dignified Freedom Fighter vibes. They did act like rockstars, though too loud, breaking furniture, staying up all night, and sleeping all day. So, we settled on names of the brothers and one half of the R&B group Jodeci, and it stuck. K-Ci and Jo-Jo were staples of our KidCrew culture: highly verbal and friendly, children and grown-ups alike loved them, and while Jo-Jo would flow inside and out like the crew, K-Ci was far too skittish to venture beyond our home's threshold. Until the Friday evening he got out. No one noticed him leave, and to this day, I have no idea what made him venture off, but whatever the case, we were awoken by the police notifying us that my sweet pumpkin spice (what I called my ginger tabby) got into the neighbor's yard and met his demise by way of the neighbors American Bully. Pain is a gross understatement for the way K-Ci's death devastated our family and through my anguish I kept thinking, I have no idea how I'm going to open on Monday morning. But as the texts came in from my crew's grown-ups explaining how they had to break the news to their children and hearing their various responses, I knew what I had to do. So I sent out a mass message notifying my clients that I would open the following day. It was unseasonably warm for early May and a beautiful cloudless sky as my crew started filtering in. As if they had sent each other a cryptic mark-making that only children under five could read, each of them came dressed up. Some wore dresses, and some wore slacks and button down tops. They brought flowers and pictures of their interpretation of my sweet kitty, and one even brought a tiny catnip which we placed on the marker I put down where he had been buried. I looked around at the displays of empathy and kindness, two of my crew were perched over the marker, and one of them said in a hushed voice, "Goodbye, K-Ci. I'll miss you." I'm not even going to lie. It was very hard to get through that moment, but I felt what I needed to feel until the feelings went away, just as I would suggest to any of them. Suddenly it hit me; it was the perfect day for a cat funeral, which consisted of me turning on Co-Co as they explored K-Ci's new resting place. When we were all gathered in the same area, we talked about what happened, and I kept it very matter of fact as I used my own imagination to process what could've possibly happened. *There was a cat-sized hole in the space* between our gate and the neighbor's yard. I reasoned that *K-Ci must've been tempted by the grass*—my cats did love to munch on grass. I continued on with my tale, imagining K-Ci slinking into the neighbor's yard where he ran into the dog, "…and the dog, he only wanted to protect his yard… He probably said, 'Get out of my yard!' But K-Ci said no, and they started to fight." I could see the kids completely captivated and could almost imagine the epic Simba and Scar-esque battle unfolding in their minds. I told them that the dog was too big, and K-Ci got hurt and died. One of my older kids cried, some asked questions. Others said nothing but sat transfixed as if they were rewatching the footage in their mind's eye.

For the next two and a half weeks, all of their play included animal fights. They were lions, tigers, apex predators, and venomous snakes. In their play, they were always beasts of prey, never the game. Like me, they wished that things had gone differently, but they had the power to make it different through their play and that was a beautiful thing.

Although I have never shared the story in full detail like I'm describing now—because I can't imagine that people would be able to get the point through my woeful gibberish, I do share the abridged version often as many families on community threads have to navigate the death of a pet with little people, and they struggle with what to say and do. And while I know the developmentally appropriate thing to say, experience is the best teacher, and if I could show up authentically in that moment and walk nine children through such an unspeakably hard conversation, well, I think I deserve to be the authority on the matter.

Pause

Can you recall the first hard topics you had to walk through with the children you share space with? What did that experience reveal about your children? What did it reveal about yourself?

Full transparency: since 2020 I've had a masterclass in navigating grief, death, and other tragedies while working with children, but, prior to that, I was a novice, wrapped up in my adult sensibilities like a comfy cocoon. Quite frankly, back then, I looked at any behavior outside of what could fit neatly into my lesson plan, not as communication but as an imposition. I loved the children that I cared for nevertheless, my relationships were transactional: let them into my home, care for them, create a playful environment, teach them some things, and send them home. Rinse and repeat. An instance that I shudder to recall happened in 2019 when I cared for a child who lost her uncle by suicide. He was young, it was sudden, and the child's mother was shattered. When my four-year-old companion came to daycare and tried to incorporate her thoughts into our morning circle, "Uncle Benny died last night." she said through pouted lips. I exchanged some niceties like "I'm sorry to hear that, babe." that undoubtedly sent the message that I'd prefer to talk about anything else and promptly redirected the conversation to a book or a song. When I "caught" her talking about it with one of her friends as they laid on their cots, I politely cut the conversation short, reminding them that it was time to give their brains a rest, thinking that she would scare her friend and give them nightmares. During lunch the following day, she shared with the crew that "Everybody dies, even our mommies and our daddies." Two children simultaneously burst into tears. Another one called out, "and grandma's too?" Before joining her distraught friends, I took it personally and placed ill-intent on the child and said, "Listen, you are making my friends sad and that's not okay."

I talked with her mother—not to offer comfort but to enlist support to keep the child from scaring the other kids around her. I did damage control when her cot-mate did have nightmares and their confused parents addressed concerns, and I would have done anything to get this family to stop exposing the daycare to their private affairs.

Pause

Let's examine the ruptures in this humbling recollection. First, I led with my fears about the cause of death and my personal inability to broach the subject with the children that I cared for. Instead of leading with curiosity, I became rigid and blocked the opportunity to step beyond my comfort threshold at every turn. Next, I worried about everyone: myself, the other children in my care, and what their grown-ups thought. By hyper-focusing on the nonessential, I created a gross oversight of the grief-stricken family and the precious child who was simply trying to make it all make sense and I wouldn't let her. I remember saying things to myself like, I wish they'd just let me do my job. If I could talk to my past self I would say, Sis. This was the job! *Let's get back to it.*

The unintentional harm we do when we are not developmentally informed is astonishing. Looking back at this display of micro-invalidation is cringeworthy to say the least, but it is necessary to disclose because it illustrates how we are all capable of mastery when we do the work. If I am here, fully committed to child advocacy in the fall of 2023, when I didn't even know that was a thing in the autumn of 2019, there is hope for all of you wherever you land on that spectrum. Having said that, growth isn't formed in a vacuum, and pedagogical maturity will not magically spring into being simply because you desire it. Your growth will demand that you are plugged in to best practice. I do not mean this in a blanket, prescriptive way. I mean that you will need to be well attuned to what is culturally and developmentally responsive and customized to the children in your environment. You will need to do your research. And in the process, you will be sure to come across the things you didn't realize you did not know.

A word of caution: make space in your heart and mind for the things that sting, because as surely as you are reading these words, you are going to find thoughts, procedures that you put in place, and behaviors that you will need to peel away. As you peel away the veil blocking your awareness, all the children you didn't serve fully or correctly will be revealed. This is going to hurt, there are no two ways around it. But the only way out is through. Give yourself grace when you get to that place of realizing what you didn't know and steel yourself with the commitment that when you know better, the children you serve will grow better.

Full Stop

When I started caring for children 23 years ago, it was before "googling that ish" was the common and preferred method of finding out information, Facebook wouldn't come out for another

4 years and Instagram was still a decade away from launching. Back then, you acquired your information from books, journals, and magazines, and the single story for educators was that we did things the way they always had been done. Though there were a few things that I felt intuitively needed to change, I couldn't value what I couldn't name so the needle moved forward, but only by inches. As I mentioned early on in the book, the advocacy that Samuel does through Honoring Childhood was pivotal in helping me reimagine a practice that centered the children in my care. I found myself with an insatiable thirst for knowledge, and thanks to books in physical and audio form, podcasts, and social media, my enlightenment was on tap.

If you are at the point in your journey where you're longing for knowledge, you have come to the right place. Continue to find a list of books, podcasts, and social media pages that will quench your intellectual thirst.

Let's move along.

Picture It: The Death Song

It was the end of the summer, the kids were playing outside on the colossal playset I'd purchased as a 12th anniversary gift, and the cicadas were deep. One four-year-old, our resident entomologist, was a fan and took to rescuing the large, scream-singing flying bugs that had gotten upended by turning them over one by one in his palm and allowing them to fly away. On one early evening, while swinging on his belly, I noticed that something had his attention, and it wasn't the grass that had been given a beating by constant trampling, slip and slide, and zero watering.

I watched as he slowly got up from his swinging position and crept over to a spot just in front of the swing. He cupped his hands, inspecting its contents, gently placed it back down on the ground in a crack of dry, depleted earth. A three-year-old friend came over and noticed what he was doing and inquired, "Are you putting it to bed?"

"No," our bug saver replied somberly. "He's already dead. I'm burying him."

For the next few days, kids gathered around the crack to inspect the cicada, stuffed into the crack like a sardine in a dirty tuxedo. It was intriguing to me how all of the younger kids came over every day and repeated what they were told, "It's dead." But each of them proceeded with caution, as if they expected it to come fluttering out of the ground, kicking and ready to keep up a lot of noise!

Little people are concrete thinkers, so phrases like it passed away, or it went to heaven mean absolutely nothing to them if they don't have a tangible representation. This cicada, in all of its cadaverous glory, was something that they could see with their own eyes and connect the fact that dead meant it didn't move, they could listen and notice that dead meant that there was no sound, no flapping of the wings, no more scream-songs for this little bugger. Finally, if they so choose, they could touch—with a stick or their fingers—and know that dead meant that it was still. It wouldn't jump up like its grateful cicada brethren that had been saved before him. This one was gonna stay put until the earth or some other animal came to claim it.

There was no big philosophical talk, kids don't need all of that, and rather than wait until it is necessary to explain death with the passing of a loved one, try explaining the process simply the next time you see something that you have no emotional ties to that is dead as the proverbial doornail. Kids will dig it, they love to learn things, and they also love to poke things with confidence when they know it won't get up and start poking back!

A few weeks after writing the cicada's death song, I received the honor of making space for a very real, very tragic death of one of my daycare babies' relatives. The relative was young, it was sudden, and my kiddo's mother was shattered. Our community mobilized and began figuring out ways in which we could best help this family that was an extension of us. I offered up drop-in days in order for the grown-ups to have time to grieve fully, and when she came to school, I let her take the lead. I did not offer up what I knew or inquire about what I didn't. During our morning play, I was pushing her on the swing, as was our morning ritual, and she looked up at me and said, "Ms. Kisa, my mommy's brother died."

I let my concern show on my face so that she would understand that this was a disturbing acknowledgement. "Yes," I said, "I'm sure that made your mommy very sad." The girl nodded, as I kept pushing her, mixing our conversation with regular *swing talk*, Do you want to go to the gate, the clouds, or the moon?

"The moon," she continued, kicking her feet straight in front of her to prevent a wobble cast by an angular push.

"There was a fire, and he fell down and he couldn't get out… and I got to play my game."

I let her trailing thoughts take over, remaining careful not to overwhelm her with my adult concern. "Oh, did you enjoy it?"

Throughout the day, my little one shared little bit of what she knew, emerging in her play,

> Then the bad guy freezes the whole fire and no people got hurt, but one of them died and he couldn't come back, but there was a superhero and he saved everybody else… also, all the superheroes from anime were there; wonder woman and Black Panther.

During story time we were talking about feelings, and she shared that her mother just wanted to lay on the couch and cry, and I offered,

> Yes…you know, when it is someone's turn to die, our heart has all of the love we felt for them inside and it hurts because we feel like it has nowhere to go, so it just comes out of the water in our eyes.

I could see my little friend thinking about what I was saying as she nodded, and I continued on. "So, when you see your mommy cry, it's just love finding somewhere to go, and that's a good thing."

I doubt that she remembers our conversation at gathering time. She may have instantly forgotten the superhero infused retelling of her uncle's fatal fire escape, but I know that there are concrete things that she may be able to hold on to like getting pushed on the swing on the fall afternoon when her uncle died. Going for a walk and collecting leaves, and even playing the game on her tablet the night before. She knew from her few years earthside what tears were. She knew hurt, and she knew how sad the thought of being lost was and how it felt to have nowhere to go. She knew the concept of love, and I hope that my willingness to provide a place for her to get away and be fully immersed in the innocence of her youth, only touching grief in a way that was safe and age appropriate, was beneficial during her four-year-old experience of death under tragic circumstances.

Same situations, different players. One thread between them: me. What changed the outcome? Four years of experience caused me to grow exponentially in my practice. I learned that sharing space is more than inviting a child into your home, and sharing space is about inviting the possibility of fellowship. It is about creating a sense of belonging that flows so well that kith become chosen kin. The humans we choose are not transactions to be exchanged. They are not written into schedules, and they're experiences to whisper about because we are afraid of the discomfort it will bring to others. Sharing space is a collective. We grieve together, we support, we empower. I'm telling you; a mindset shift makes a hell of a difference.

Whether it is between colleagues, provider and grown-up caregiver, or provider and child, relating to race, injustice, vulnerability, advocacy, death, or scary times, the importance of conversation is vital in environments shared with children. These discussions call for a high level of expertise.

Pause:

Knowledge and experience are not the same. You can go through years of higher education and acquire the degrees to document that you are qualified in the field, but it is the successful application of what you have learned that makes you experienced.

Samuel, conversations, and consent are your areas of expertise. I'm curious how many years have you worked and does that match how many years of experience you have in the field? And during what part of your practicum did conversations and consent to honoring childhood's toolkit?

4

Conversation, Kindness, and Consent

This is one of the most important pieces of this play, and it is something that was a major part of my own journey through understanding and encouraging this type of play.

One thing that I tell educators and families all the time is this: conversation is everything! We should be continually having conversations with our children—even as infants. They need to be able to not only understand how communication works in a general sense, but they need to understand that the words they speak have power and they have the ability to speak about the way they are feeling, what they want, what they don't want, and more. True conversations should be happening all the time in our classrooms, and when I say true, I mean an actual conversation where you and the child or children are engaged in communication. Not the usual, "What did you make?" "Oh it's so great!" back and forth. A conversation where you are talking and listening and caring about what the child has to say to you.

These conversations fit perfectly into what we are discussing in terms of weapon play. If you remember my story from the introduction of this book, you will remember that a conversation with my students was what really set me on the track of rethinking my "no" when it comes to weapon play. But it wasn't the easiest thing to do—I had to do some self-reflection to prepare myself to be

DOI: 10.4324/9781032679808-5

ready to have an actual conversation with them about this. I had to make sure that I was not going into the conversation with my own ideas leading the way. I had to make sure that I was coming into this conversation with the goal of just talking and listening. What was interesting about this conversation was that when I first brought it up with the children, it took me about ten minutes to convince them that they were not in trouble. When I first told them that I noticed that they were using sticks as weapons and I wanted to know more about that, their first response was "no we weren't." This gave me pause and caused me to do even further reflection to think if I had done something that would cause the children to automatically think they were in trouble. I told you there was a lot of self-reflection in this work, right? Once I was able to convince the children that they were not in trouble and that I did, in fact, just want to talk to them about this, the conversation was able to open up and we were able to connect deeper about this and begin to discuss how we could make this type of play work for us.

What Conversation Teaches Children

When we engage in meaningful conversations with children, we are giving them an opportunity to be heard and take part in something very important. If we were to look around at child-care programs around the country, we would not see a lot of true and meaningful conversations. What we would see a lot more of most likely are one-sided discussions where the teacher or adult is the one doing the talking and, most of the time, the talking comes with a goal of getting the child to do something rather than having an actual conversation and understanding with the child. That is honestly what most of the discussions end up being in early childhood: a way for the adult to talk and the child to listen. This stems from years and years of children being devalued and not respected as anything more than a small human that needs to be obedient and listen to adults in order to be "good." People do not tend to truly care about what children think or believe or have to say because they do not see children as equals. That is a thought process that needs to be shifted. We need to stop

How do you view children?

thinking of ourselves as somehow "above" the children or better than them. We need to stop thinking of children as people with no thoughts or ideas. We need to start thinking of children as equal beings to us and a part of our connection to the world around us. We need to start giving children the respect that we so often demand from them. This is the first step towards having meaningful conversations with the children we work with.

How to Do It

So, I know what you are probably thinking: yeah that all sounds great, but how do I go about having the actual conversation about weapon play with my children? It is really quite simple, if you are willing.

First, reflect. You need to spend time thinking about your own thoughts and feelings about this type of play. You need to be able to not let your own thoughts and feelings run the conversation or lead the children to any type of idea that is not their own. (How many times do we see children doing or saying something just because an adult or teacher did?) We want to make sure that we are encouraging them to think for themselves. It is, of course, important and necessary to speak about your own feelings during this conversation, but you want to make sure that you are not pushing those ideas onto the children. (It is the same reason that I try to not act scared when the children bring me a bug—I don't want to push my fears onto them, right?).

Second, just ask the question. Ask them what they like about playing this way. Ask them how it makes them feel. Encourage them to answer honestly. Remember a true conversation is when you actually care about what they are saying. Have a conversation with them stemming from this question. Include your own thoughts here too. When I had this conversation with my students, this is where I said something like,

> I get that it is really fun to you and I want you to enjoy yourselves, but sometimes this can make me a bit nervous or uncomfortable. Can you understand that? But I am wanting to work through those feelings with you.

(Imagine how it would have felt to have an adult speak to you like this when you were a child!). The important thing is to let the conversation flow naturally. If you need to give it a little push, go ahead. The goal of this conversation should be to get the children's thoughts and ideas about this type of play and to decide as a collective if this is something that you can continue to do. (We will talk about how to have this conversation if you are working in a community where this type of play would not be appropriate or safe in a later chapter.)

Lastly, decide how to move forward regarding this type of play TOGETHER. This is the important part. Whatever you decide should be decided on as a collective. I know we are used to making decisions for the children, but it is important to ensure that they have a say in what is going on as well. Talk with them about what it could look like if you all decided that this type of play was safe in your program. Talk with them about what they think needs to happen in order for everyone to feel safe and heard. Involving the children in all aspects of this conversation and decision really gives them that sense of power and that what they have to say and what they think really matters.

Consent

What was great about this specific conversation for me was that it naturally brought up the topic of consent with the children. The idea of consent was something that I had been wanting to teach the children about for some time, but I admit I was having a hard time figuring out just the right way to do it. I don't know about you, but sometimes an idea can seem so "big" that it can be difficult for us to think about how we could teach it to the children. This was one of those ideas. I knew that it was important to teach the children about consent and that they have the power to say no, right? We know there are so many reasons why this is important for children to learn—it can help them to feel confident, it can help them to understand that they are in control, it can help them to recognize signs of abuse and be able to speak up, and it can help them be better prepared for their lives. Again, if we are reflecting on our own lives, we may be able to see how the lack of knowledge surrounding consent may have led us into some toxic and not so great relationships because we did not feel we had the power to say no or to demand the things we need out of people. (I am mostly talking to myself, but I am hopeful someone out there will also understand this!) Most of us grew up with the idea that if we say "no" to anyone-especially an adult—that we were being disrespectful. So we learn to just say "yes" no matter what. Is that what we want for these children now? I surely don't. That is why I knew this topic of consent was something that I NEEDED to teach the children. And I was over the moon when it was able to be brought up organically in our conversations about weapon play.

While we were discussing what this type of play could look like in our classroom, the children began talking about making sure that other people want to play and feel safe before we start playing and checking in throughout the play to make sure everyone is still ok with it. That's consent! They also talked about what to do if someone says they don't want to play anymore— we stop, allow that person to move on to something else, then start playing again. That's consent! It was an amazing thing for me to hear coming from the children, and it just reminded me that sometimes, adults think too much about something and we should just let the children handle it!

We were able to take this idea of consent and apply it to other parts of our classroom and our days. It started to bleed over into all we did. "Can I sit here and watch you draw?" "Can I sit on your lap?" "Can I give you a hug?" etc. An important piece of this is you engaging in it as well. We as adults need to make sure that we are asking for consent from the children before we do something and accepting the answer they give. We also need to encourage the children to ask us before they do something and give them an honest answer. So if a child comes up and wants to sit in our lap, for instance, we can say "can you ask me first please?" and we can also say "I don't want that right now". It is important for children to understand that the answer is sometimes "no" and that is ok. It is ok for them to say no, and it is ok for someone to tell them no. It is all about the power. It is all about showing children that they have the power to say no. This is a part of treating children as equals. We need to do a better job of understanding that children do not owe us anything. Teaching them that they have the power to consent or not to things happening to them is an important step in their development and will be something that they carry with them long after they leave us.

Does thinking about children saying no to you make you uncomfortable? That's ok! Again, we have been taught our whole lives that children are less than and that they don't have the right to question or say no to an adult. That is how we were raised most likely and that is how we are taught to view children now. It takes a lot of work and reflection to get past that. But the important thing is that you try!

A Note on Consent from Kisa

One of the greatest teachers I had on the magic of consent came from a rising five-year-old. I cared for this child from the time she was 1.5 and had a wonderful relationship with her—we talked, laughed, and shared little insiders with one another—it honestly set the bar for relationships that I want to have with the children in my care. But guess what? This child did not like for me to touch her. I mean, no hugs, no rubs, no hand holding—*nada*. When I first noticed, she was still relatively small, and I thought it was just that we were getting to know one another. Then, as she got older, I would blow it off like, oh, she's just having big feelings. She wouldn't avoid your touch like the plague if she was regulated. When she was regulated and did in fact avoid my touch like the plague, it was hard not to take it personally. I worried that I was doing something wrong. I worried that our relationship had some fracture that I didn't see. I worried that she didn't like me as much as I liked her. Then I stopped. I thought long and hard about the time we spent together and how she would always engage me with conversation. How she enjoyed knowing what I had eaten for dinner the night before, or what I was going to do after she left in the evening. How she asked to join in my personal play—if I was doing a puzzle, cooking, or creating. This child didn't dislike me, she just didn't want to be touched, and that was okay!

Through this experience I learned how to give, not what I wanted but what was needed. If a child falls, I observe: the child is rocking back and forth and cradling their wounded knee. I assess: Do they require assistance—what does that look like? Do they need their hurt cleaned? Does the hurt require ointment and/or a bandage? If they are crying, do they need a tissue? Next, I focus my attention: What is the child saying? This can be communicated through words or body cues. The child who wants physical touch to be a part of the consolation package will either run up to me and bury their head in my leg, hold out their arms to be picked up, or come to me and dissolve into my lap. If they don't offer those gestures, then I *ask* before rushing in and invading their space and prepare myself for the reality that the answer could be no, and, as Samuel stated above, no is okay. Finally, I pause—which is how we reflect in real time—and ask myself, "what does this child need?" Not every child needs a hug or to be pulled in close. Some children just want to know that you are there if *they need you*. I borrowed a saying from my good friend and West African dance instructor, Mama Donna, which is, we must look, listen, and think. It is an easy assessment for little people to apply so I incorporated it into our crew's lexicon. Through working with my young mentor, I learned how to put looking, listening, and thinking into practice. I developed the ability to see beyond my worldview, tap into the needs of the child, and consider how my behavioral language supports or discourages consent.

Words from Kisa Weapon Play Reframe: A How To

Samuel, indulge me as I pop in with my .02 cents on the subject. You are absolutely right; it is quite simple—once you do the hard work of moving beyond the confines of your current mindset!

Educators, think of it this way: in the typical culturally responsive classroom, you will find all the markers of *mirrors* which ensure all the children can feel seen and *windows* that allow children to view another's perspective. If we step back—so far back that we're out of the way to make room for play, then we are preparing space for that fundamental third step in cultivating a self-affirming practice: opening the sliding glass doors. When it comes to difficult topics such as power, conflict, and scary times, our children lack the verbiage and complexity of thought to express when something is overwhelming, confusing, or frightening to them and opening that sliding glass door will allow the children to relay those messages to you. Remember the practitioner's golden rule: *All behavior is communication*! Instead of viewing weapon play, war play, death play, and rough-and-tumble play through a lens of outward aggression or inward discomfort, I encourage you to look at it through the lens of quiet observation: What can you document about the play? What feelings does a particular form of play conjure up for you? What do those feelings feel like in your body? And what conversations can you have during your gathering times that give space for sorting out what is going on? Mining these behaviors for meaning may be tough for an emerging reflective practitioner, but it will not be fruitless because weapon play isn't simply mindless brutality, but it is experiential learning gold!

Picture It: The Predicament at Pickup

A grown-up caregiver enters a home child care at pickup time and becomes visibly distressed as she observes her child chasing a friend around the kitchen table. The child is pretending to shoot another child who is the "bad guy". His two thumbs, the hammer and his two index fingers, the barrel. The grown-up sighs as she pulls the child's coat from their cubby.

Grown-up: ugh, we have just hit the "everything is a weapon" phase. We were trying to avoid the words. "Gun," and "shoot," but they're getting into Nerf play, and it's made it a lot harder…I feel like it's a losing battle.

Any provider that has been around for more than a year knows that the silence that stands between what your grown-up stakeholder is feeling, what you know as an educator, and what you plan to say when the difficult topics arise feels impenetrable, but I literally had only seconds to respond thoughtfully before the silence became awkward and doubt crept in. *Deep breath*, I remind myself. I run through my handy-dandy advocate's toolkit and ask myself three questions before responding: *Is it helpful? Is it necessary? Is it kind?*

And go!

Me: Can I offer you a slightly different perspective? Maybe it isn't a losing battle but a battle not worthy of a fight. (Kind and necessary: check, check)

Weapon play is as age appropriate as fairy/princess play, dinosaur play, and monster play. But we grown-ups never worry that our children will go to school and eat their classmates a lá

Penelope Rex, or that they will grow up and try to demand their rightful position in Buckingham Palace. (Necessity mixed with humor, if you have a knack for that, never hurts.)

We worry about weapon play because of what it means to *us*. *We* know of the carnage. *We* know of the devastation, but that is *our* burden to carry for now and not theirs to inherit just yet.

There it is…true advocacy. I had to work my way up to it, but I delivered in the 11th hour! No one said that standing up for what is developmentally informed and responsive would be easy. Sometimes you're going to worry about offending the parent, that they won't understand or, worse, flat out disagree with what you are telling them, but you're going to find that champion of children inside of you and let it speak for you when you feel that you cannot. Speak up for children when no one else will. Speak up for children when you have to be a renegade. Speak up for children when your palms are sweaty, your mouth is dry, and the butterflies won't stop fluttering. No one will know any of those things, but everyone will hear what you say, and if we're all lucky, what you say will make a difference.

Picture It: Caregiver Conversation with Kisa

Picture it: I'm walking down the corridor of a nondescript pre-school at the end of a long day when I bump into a pre-k colleague, Ms. Ginny, from the room across the hall. After exchanging a few pleasantries, Ms. Brenda notes that she observed my students (3's and new 4's) as they played a "shooting" game earlier in the day.

MS. GINNY: You aren't worried that playing games like that aren't good for them?

> For context, Ms. Ginny is biracial. And although her mother is black, her fair skin and light eyes make her racial identity appear as if she is either white or of pan-ethnic descent.

> I've known Ms. Ginny for a long time and understand that although our teaching approaches are totally different, she's a fierce advocate of the predominantly black and brown children that we serve in the West-Side Preschool where we work and she is also always up for a respectful challenge, and on this day, I would be the one to provide the thoughtful discourse.

ME: No, they're just pretending. What is there to worry about?

MS. GINNY: I'm concerned with pretend gun play leading to desensitization—the same way the consumption of culture in TV and games do it. Shooting imaginary blasters at monsters isn't my worry. Shooting imaginary guns at people, though, is where I draw the line.

> Ms.Ginny's perspective isn't wrong, but I see an in for my tried-and-true argument and seize the opportunity to deliver!

ME: It's that part that has me stumped. If a four-year-old has an imaginary friend, we don't pathologize them and worry that they will suffer from psychosis. If they tell us they're going to "eat us up," we don't fear future cannibalism. If two children are wrestling in the grass, we don't think they're going to live out their days being dragged out of brawl room fights. Yet, we worry incessantly about the meaning behind why a child is pointing, aiming, and shooting and what that will mean for them later on in life. I just don't get it.

I then explain the hypocrisy I would feel banning weapon play in my classroom when I allowed my children to wrestle and play imaginative games with weapons and toy guns at home.

Ginny looks concerned but prepared to counterstrike and responds: in my home, we're extremely strict about weapon play—with caveats. If it is something that looks in no way real, with "loud colors," they can play with it at *other people's houses.* We will not own the toys ourselves in our home.

Her big green eyes stare earnestly in my direction, and I know I better have my listening ears on and up because she's about to say something I *need* to hear.

MS. GINNY: If the toy looks realistic, they may not touch it. Period. My nephews are Black and are not allowed to either—we know from real-life events like Tamir Rice that their bodies are seen as threatening even at a young age. While my kids are brown and one is white passing, we teach them these racial issues from day 1. If my nephews can experience it, my kids can learn about it. If their cousins cannot safely play with these toys, we don't play in solidarity.

Pause

Though Ginny and I both had valid perspectives, and both led with curiosity, the figurative dance we were doing was unlikely to find common ground because common ground in this debate is hopelessly entangled in the middle. My stance was an objective one, identical to the stance I want educators to take when rethinking the divergent ways that children use their imagination to create meaning of the world around them. Ginny's stance was subjective, intentionally focused on the children who are omitted from the conversation when speaking objectively. Both *what*—the social issues that plague us as a society—and *why*—adult triggers, issues, and discomfort—are vital points to consider in our quest to create a liberated learning environment that is culturally responsive and trauma informed. But the arguments are binary in thinking: either we allow it or we don't, and it doesn't make space for us to examine the nuances, find places that allow flexibility, and discover the opportunity to reframe our approach.

In my mind, I know that if we are developmentally informed and striving to become developmentally responsive, we have the responsibility of acknowledging the things that we view through an adult lens that impact a child's innocence. On the other hand, as the mother of three black males identifying children, my heart and my conscience will always mirror Ginny's and lead with *what*.

This is the tough part for educators of color, or educators who work with People of the Global Majority children. You have to straddle the fence between what you know is best and what you know is *safe*. But if we employ a nonbinary approach, we clear space for *both-and.*

My boys were 11, 13, and 16 the year Tamir Rice was killed. They didn't grow up in a wonderland, but they were sheltered enough that they were allowed to play cops and robbers and other weapon play games without issue. But after the lynching of a young black child for playing in the park with a toy gun, my entire thought process changed. I remember the day when I got a call that my middle son was being detained by the police at the neighborhood convenience store and I needed to come and pick him up. I cannot even describe the feeling of fear that filled my body. Luckily, the convenient store was just around the corner, and I can't tell you whether I walked, ran, or teleported, but I know that I was there fast. When I arrived to see my son unharmed, smiling, and talking with the officer, I was utterly confused. His friends were there too, all looking guilty, but no worse for wear. The officer came to the car and explained what happened.

He led with, "You've got a good kid." and then he went on to tell me, "It seems the boys had a BB gun and were playing a game of chase on their bikes..." my mind went blank. I honestly could not believe what I was hearing. He continued, "there were no bb's in it, and it had the cap on, but several people called the cops, and we know how this could've gone under different circumstances."

I did.

The other circumstances that this well-meaning, black police officer was referring to is what could have happened if my 6-ft tall, black child had been speeding through the street on his bike just a mile west of the village where we lived. Had the friends he was chasing looked like him as they sped down those streets along with him, this story would have had an alternate ending. I felt sick to my stomach, and furious, and relieved all at once. We had *the talk* with all of our boys—for those of you who are not aware, the talk is not referring to the conversation that parents have with their adolescent children about the birds and the bees. It is the heartbreaking conversation that black parents have with their children about the dangers that they may encounter when faced with racism in the world or with law enforcement and what measures they should take to deescalate the situation in effort to make it home alive. They knew about social injustice and how their size and the color of their skin made them a threat in the gaze of racist eyes. Did my child think he was absolved of that reality because his friends happened to be white? If I could've dragged my child home by his ear that night, I would have. I remember him not understanding my outrage. He kept telling me that nothing happened, and the officers weren't upset and no one got in trouble, and it was just a toy.

Just a toy.

Looking at it from where I stand now, I understand his confusion. He was looking at it through a lens of his youth, his innocence, his naivety, and his partially developed prefrontal cortex. I was looking at it through a lens of fear and lived experience. Fear that my children weren't safe in their own bodies. Fear that pretense of safety in their neighborhood would be dangerous for them the moment that they stepped outside of it. Fear that his trust in the police, who were the exception to an unjust rule, could prove disastrous once he came across the many working within a broken system. I was outraged because my son couldn't see those things with me, and I was simultaneously sickened by the thought of how susceptible to harm he would be because of it.

This is why distinguishing facts from feelings are essential tools to carry in our toolkits! Those feelings, however valid, may have felt real and may have been true for unspeakable numbers of mothers with sons who met a tragic fate, but this was neither my reality nor my truth. What was real? My son was 14, his behavior was careless, but it wasn't beyond the scope of typical teenage carelessness. He was shielded by the fact that he was a juvenile in a suburb with a police force with ties to the community, and though not void of discriminatory behavior, they were a far cry from the broken systems that housed officers like the one who lynched Laquon McDonald during the spring of the same year. What was true? Fear hadn't had a chance to take hold of my son, and so he saw things, not under the weight of living in a black body. He saw them through the eyes of a 14-year-old child. How scary for me but how lucky it was that he was able to navigate life without the dread that his father and I carried in our bodies.

My fear gave me unreasonable expectations, and those unreasonable expectations sent the message to my child that he wasn't safe. He wasn't safe when the police officer was serving and protecting. He wasn't safe riding a bike in the neighborhood. He wasn't safe playing risky games, and although his friends were safe doing all of the above, he wasn't safe because those friends were white, and he happened to be black. I'm just glad that at that point of time he was too rebellious to pick up on the messages that I was inadvertently sending. But eventually, that message of fear was.

So, what is real and true for you? Maybe you serve children who live in high crime areas. Are your feelings unintentionally sending messages of fear to those little bodies? Are you sending messages that they are unsafe? If you have, I get it. But here's the thing, now we have the opportunity to do things differently. Does that mean that we let our black and brown children run freely in public spaces with toy weapons? Unfortunately, it doesn't. But that also doesn't mean that we ban real and pretend weapon play. Our new outlook will make room for both-and. Our BIPOC children have the right to joy. They have the right to use their imagination. *And* it is an absolute necessity that we are mindful of place and space. Knowing when and where it is appropriate to play these games is a matter of safety, and implementing the practice of both-and in all learning spaces is a great way to infuse social justice within the culture of your environment. The gift we give our BIPOC babies is the space to safely belong in their own childhood, and the gift we give their white classmates is a window into a world different from their own. Is there a gift for the black educator with life experiences that make both-and a struggle? Although it won't always feel like it, the answer is yes. Through both-and we will learn how to hand down knowledge without fear, and when you are tasked with informing the young during scary times, that is an invaluable gift to be given.

Samuel, tackling both-and requires finesse and is something that requires deep understanding, and cultural sensitivity. I'm curious, have you ever had *the talk* with the children in your classes? If so, how would you handle balancing what is safe with what you know to be developmentally informed?

Teacher Toolkit

Reflections!

Remember:
Two things can be true.

5

Weapon Play in Your Community

Something that we want to make very clear in this book is that our goal for you after reading this book is not to go back into your program and give all the children toy guns and sticks and let them all do weapon play. The goal of this book is to get us to think a little bit differently and a little bit deeper about this type of play and our feelings about it. If you decide that weapon play is something that works for your program or classroom, great! But we also understand that this type of play may not be appropriate or safe for every program. There are many programs and communities where this type of play would not be safe, appropriate, or fitting.

My husband, Perry, grew up on the South Side of Chicago, much like Kisa, and when I began talking about this idea of weapon play, he was very uncomfortable with it and said that he wasn't sure if it was a good thing for children to play. I asked him why, and he told me about his childhood and the community he grew up in where these types of things were happening in real time and in real life around him and his schoolmates. This is true for a lot of us—and a lot of our programs. Many programs may be operating in communities where violence is a part of daily life for the children and families that they serve. In those cases, allowing the children to participate in play where they are shooting and killing each other may not be something that is allowed—or should be. However, even in these instances and in these communities where educators may see fit to ban

DOI: 10.4324/9781032679808-6

this type of play, there is something very important that should still be allowed and encouraged—the conversation about this type of play.

Let's think about it this way: children who live in communities where violence and weapons are a normal aspect of their lives are possibly dealing with a great deal of trauma, both realized and not, because of that. Their parents and families may quite possibly be surviving through that very same trauma. The spaces that we create for children and families should be spaces where they feel safe, supported, and cared for. When families and children are living through any sort of trauma, it is usually not spoken about much in the home, right? We want to shield our children from the bad things in the world so even if they see those bad things outside, we don't want to bring anymore of it inside our home, so we don't discuss it and we focus on happier things in our home. But children and adults need somewhere to work through that trauma. They need somewhere to talk about it—talk about their feelings, their fears, and their emotions. We need to create that space for them—and for ourselves.

A note on current events:

We can see the importance of children using play to work through trauma that they are experiencing when we look at migrant children who have been detained by ICE, children in war torn countries, and children who have experienced some of these major world tragedies and warfare.

So, let's take some time to reflect on your own practice and your own community.

Play-Based Programming is Trauma Informed Care Play-Based
—Ana Valle Rivera

For much of my life, even years into my time as a provider, I equated Montessori schools with privilege. The single story that people in my neck of the woods told me was that Montessori schools were all white walls, baskets, and beige. The children there got to do what they wanted, and their teachers never said no. Boy, were we misinformed. Imagine my surprise when I found out that Montessori schools run a pretty structured ship, and the absolute shock when I discovered that the Casa Dei Bambini, the first school that Maria Montessori opened, was created to care for neglected, malnourished, profoundly impoverished, and traumatized children. Maria Montessori took the forgotten, the discarded, and the "undesirable" children from an overpopulated, destitute, and high crime area and created a practice in which they thrived. What'd she do in this practice? She let them play.

Samuel, your writing makes me think about childhood in the midst of conflict. Whether the conflict is centralized to neighborhoods like the one Perry and I grew up in, found in detention centers, tent cities of migrants, or trudging among the rubble, dazed, and confused after a bombing, children are still children, and though one might think that the threat of violence, displacement, detainment, and war would diminish the desire to play, children have to find a way to take in what is going on around them, even during horrific events. And once those children get to even a sliver of safety, they're going to need the space to process what they have experienced, and they will inevitably do that through their play.

When I was still in elementary school, a common way to protect your block was to stand on its corner. My older brothers' friend and neighborhood block hugger was one of them. Everyday my mother pulled up to the stop sign at the top of the hill where we'd always find him in the same spot, literally perched above the mailbox. And every day my mother would tell him it was a bad idea. He'd smile and promise her he'd leave, but he didn't, and eventually his enemies knew where to find him and shot him off of his post. I remember hearing my brothers retelling the story of how he stumbled towards safety. But more than that, I remember playing a game of hopscotch over the blood-stained sidewalk on our way to school the next morning and doing the same hop again at the end of the school day. I can vividly remember the way the blood looked: blotches in a single line, then a dried pool that disappeared into the grass then reappeared on another piece of sidewalk then like connect the dots: crime scene edition. The group of children, my twin, and I walked with speculated how the blood got there: *Somebody's nose was bleeding. It was a dog.* One girl, who stayed houses away from where the drive-by occurred said somberly, "My mama told me somebody got shot last night, and that's his blood." The crowd erupted, "No, they didn't!" One schoolmate protested. "It was a dog!" another chimed in. My twin and I knew she was right, but neither of us came to her defense. Maybe because it was easier to imagine the blood having come from something as harmless as a stray's run in with a broken bottle than what it actually was. No one came out and washed the blood off the sidewalk. Every day small groups of children walked back and forth over it, and twice a day I hopped across. We began watching for dog sightings and made up little stories about how it was probably healing. Finally, after a couple of days it rained hard enough to lift much of the stains from the concrete and like that, it was onto the next grade school adventure. Looking back at this childhood memory as an adult, I wonder how many of those children wouldn't allow themselves to know what we were all walking over? I wonder how many of them were like me and my twin and preferred to pretend it was something else? I guess we'll never know.

I imagine that in the midst of severe conflict, play wouldn't look like children playing tag amidst the rubble and might be safest in the mind and look similar to our imaginary wounded dog.

6

Weapon Play during Frightening Times

The world right now is a scary place. We see almost every day on the news some new horrific act of violence or war. Honestly, this is a reason why I choose not to even watch the news—it is filled with so much sadness, death, and worry. And as much as we may try to shield our children from this, we can't shield them from everything. So, it becomes a frightening world for us all. Now, due to these feelings of fear that can rise up for us, the topic of weapon play may be even further from our minds than before. Seeing tragedies occurring in schools makes us feel like we may want to keep any form of that far far away from our classroom and program. It is a very sensitive time for all of us. Again, we want to reiterate that our goal with this book is not to get you to allow weapon play in your program—it is to get you to think differently and reflect on your lived experiences and how those can influence and inform your practice with the children that you serve. Just like the community you live and work in can inform your practice based on what the experiences of the folx there are, the community you live in and the reactions and feelings of yourself and those around to what is happening in the world can also inform your practice as it relates to weapon play.

The important thing to remember again is that it is not imperative that you allow weapon play in your classroom or

DOI: 10.4324/9781032679808-7

program because as we have seen, that might not be appropriate. However, it is imperative that you offer a space where children can and are encouraged to speak about their feelings about the world around in a safe way. This is also important to think about for yourself. Sometimes the work that we do with children to help guide them and support them can also be healing work for ourselves and our inner child.

> Sometimes the work we do with children to help guide them and support them can also be healing work for ourselves and our inner child.

Remember, weapon play may not be appropriate for your community, classroom, or program. But the conversation surrounding it and giving the space for children to explore those ideas is appropriate—we may just need to do some work on ourselves first, right?

So, how do we talk to children about tragedy? This is something that I am sure that a lot of us have been grappling with in the last few years. Not just the horrible tragedies that we see in schools and grocery stores, but the horrendous acts committed against our black neighbors, and the ongoing war and unrest around the world, then add the pandemic to that? It is a lot. We want to offer children a safe space where they can talk these things out, but how do we do that? Well first, we need to remind ourselves that it is ok to be overwhelmed, sad, scared, frustrated, and just not ok. A lot of times we may feel like we have to be strong for the children all the time, but we don't. It is actually important that the children see us not be ok because that will show them that it is ok and the cycle of feeling like we have to be strong no matter what may end. Think about it like this as a reflection—why do we feel the need to be strong no matter what and hide our feelings or emotions? Could it be because that is what we saw in the adults we were around growing up? Could it be because that is what we were told to do? And all of that has carried with us, right? So, if we don't want the same thing for these children now (and we shouldn't), then we need to let them know that it is ok to not be ok.

Second, we need to be able to speak honestly with the children about how we feel. Sometimes, it may be hard for children to open up about tragic events that they see on TV or that they have witnessed in their lives, but having an adult they know, and trust open the conversation up and show vulnerability can be a really helpful tool to help support them in speaking up as well.

Third, just allow the conversation to flow where it will. I have learned throughout my years in the field that going into anything with children with a set outcome or goal can be frustrating—because children will do what they want! That is why I have learned to go into any conversation I have with children with no expectation other than an open dialogue. I don't want to go in thinking "I am going to get them to talk about their feelings and open up to me!" because that could lead me to push them into a conversation that they are just not ready to have yet so that I can fulfill the goals I have set out for them myself.

If we work to create spaces where conversation is valued and encouraged, where children are supported and feel seen and safe, and where all feelings are celebrated and worked through together, we can give children that space that we may have needed when we were younger and also give them that space they need to help them work through the traumatic events of the world they are living in. It is important to remember that we do not want to shy away from tough conversations. We understand that these conversations can be difficult to have for a variety of reasons, but shying away from them will not help either us or the children learn how to positively handle and work through issues, problems, fears, worries, or feelings. Remember that all we do and show the children now are going to be things that they carry with them for the rest of their lives. When we spent our time reflecting on our past in this book, we were able to recognize that a lot of who we are today comes from the experiences that we had as children. So if we know that that is the case, then we know that the experience we provide for the children today will help mold them into who they will be as adults. That is a very big responsibility and one that we should not take lightly.

Just remember, the best thing you can do for children is to work on and heal yourself first and then offer them spaces that you wish you would have had as a child. You know, a lot of times I talk about "remembering our why"—and I think that now is a good space to talk about it. So often in our work, we get so bogged down by so many things—making sure the children are safe, communicating with the families, remembering to fill out accident reports, performing assessments, dealing with co-workers, and more—that we oftentimes can forget the reason why we started working with children to begin with. This can lead us to consider leaving our programs or the field as a whole. Believe me, I have been there too. There were many, many times when I was at the end of my rope, feeling so overwhelmed with keeping up with everything that had to be done (licensing, family communication and concerns, safety, behaviors that were deemed challenging, etc.) that I just said to myself, "is this even worth it?" We already know that folx who work in the early education field are undervalued and severely underpaid. So it became quite easy for me to just say, "forget this, I'll go work at Target and make the same money." How many of you have been there? I am assuming quite a few of you who are reading this. This is why it is so important for us to remember our why! I did and it is what kept me motivated to keep pushing forward and keep doing what I could do to give children the experience and space that I wanted to.

Here is a great tip that really helped me in remembering my why:

> | spend time in reflection to remind yourself what it is that drew you to working with children. Once you have that-your WHY!- write it down somewhere and put it somewhere that you will see it each day. That way when you wake up in the morning and are feeling defeated about going into the classroom that day or when you come home from a long day feeling stressed and overwhelmed, you can look at that little note and hopefully get some

encouragement. (We will talk more about the importance of encouragement from each other in a later chapter.).

That is what I did. It was as simple as that. I reflected on my reason for working with children—I want to give children a safe and supportive space to discover who they truly are with no judgments—and I wrote it down on a little sticky note and placed in on my mirror and was able to look at it and reflect on it each day, and it really helped me to feel not only more encouraged but more connected to my work.

Another great thing to think about when you are thinking and reflecting on your why is to think about *what is your goal for the children in your program*? What is it that you want them to gain from their time with you? How do you want them to feel being with you? What do you want them to take with them when they move on from your classroom or program? This can be another great piece of self-reflection that can really help inform your practice—especially on those days when you feel overwhelmed or like you are a bad teacher (we've all been there! I can't tell you how many days I would come home and think to myself "I should have said that differently" or "I shouldn't have responded that way").

The experiences we provide for the children today will help mold them into who they will be as adults.

Words from Kisa

We can all touch and agree that there wasn't a living soul who was not impacted by the global pandemic of 2020. No schools, no libraries, no parks, no friends. Life as we knew it quite literally stopped, but injustice didn't get the memo. And what was already a frightening time, became wrought with civil unrest. Stores were boarded up to avoid looting. Windows shuttered. Marching in the streets. Samuel, when I think back to that time, it feels like a page ripped from some dystopian tale, but this was our real life, and I don't think anyone escaped without acquiring at least a remnant of the collective trauma. That includes the youngest among us. Children didn't stop being children because the voraciousness of COVID-19 took precedence. They didn't stop being children when necks were being kneeled on and anguished citizens took to the streets in protest. They were there: witnessing, listening, and feeling.

Both of us were in practice with children during that time, Samuel, and I don't know how long your learning environment was on lockdown, but ours was closed for all of two days. This is a part of the childcare burnout that we don't talk about enough. If you had families who were essential workers, then, by default, so were you. Since my clientele at the time consisted of a majority of healthcare professionals, there wasn't really a second thought to whether I would remain open. I took enough time to prepare my family and my crew families, and I was back open the following Monday morning. For any other care-workers who shared space with children in the 2019–2020 school year, you know that there were children prior to COVID, and children post COVID. The decline in wellness was undeniable. There was a spike in meltdowns and disagreements, and there were actual instances of physicality, something that only happened rarely with my small crew. Like many caregivers in the country, I worried about the welfare of the children I cared for and wondered what I could do to prevent future trauma.

Looking back on that time through a developmentally informed lens however, I can see that the children were trying to make sense of it all: the uncertainty, the fragility, the fear, and anger. Those complexities expressed through behavior looked very much like child-sized chaos, but what it was communicating was that as a result of a world in its reactive state, many basic needs were going unmet. How do you fulfill the need for human warmth when physical contact isn't allowed? How do you help someone feel secure when everyone is sheltering in place? How do you maintain a sense of belonging when many of your friends have vanished, you can't visit your loved ones, and you can't even see the faces of your caregivers and the friends around you who remain? It's nearly impossible to feel free in the midst of social upheaval and constant talk overheard about death and dying. No human warmth, no emotional safety, no belonging means that any desire to do anything beyond survival is completely shut down. Why on earth did we expect our children to behave in any other way?

The turning point came when I had all of my crew head out to our tiny backyard one afternoon. I was grasping at straws, really. I thought back to my own childhood and how safety prevented us from being able to play beyond the front of our house. There, on that small patch of land, we designed universes, and to my surprise, that is exactly what my tiny crew did too.

By the time the lockdown lifted and we were able to return to nature walks, the kids ran free across chalk filled sidewalks listing the names of slain victims of police injustice and racially incited violence: Ahmaud Arbery, Breonna Taylor, George Floyd…they stopped to admire, touch, and smell flowers in gardens with signs that read BLACK LIVES MATTER, and they waved at neighbors, eager to see proof of life through windows decorated with messages that HATE HAS NO HOME HERE. Even if no one uttered a word, it was all around them. Scary talk of guns, and broken glass, fires, and turned over cars. And that really big, really scary word: murder.

One afternoon, my little friend sat fiddling his fingers as he looked out into the distance. We were relaxing after a picnic as the rest of the crew ran in the field outside of our neighborhood park. He started to say, "Last night, we talked about slavery," which sounded more like, *wast night we tawked about swavery*, and brought a bit of levity to what I knew was going to be a heavy topic. Without looking at me directly, my three-year-old companion tried to collect his thoughts. He fought out the words, *and a Bwack Man was be kiwed by a powice office*r. By this time a couple of the other children had gathered on our blanket to catch their breath or get a drink of water. I asked him what he thought about that and he told me he felt scared and he didn't want them to come to his house. Suddenly, he was up, slashing the sky in ninja pose to show me what he would do if those scary police officers showed up at his door. I said, "You'd get them good, wouldn't you?" and he smiled and agreed. In a split second, this three-year-old was able to take a big, frightening topic and guard himself against those fears with his imaginary sword and fighting pose. This is the magic lost when we reject the notion of weapon play. We deny that comfort that a child needs that we as adults cannot give them. We can't shield them from their big scary thoughts, especially when we're afraid of the boogey man ourselves. I think about that afternoon often because at that time, weapon play of any kind was still forbidden, but it was something about the purity in that moment. The innocence that was shown through so clearly and that helped me get it that day, and I'm so grateful that I chose connection over correction in that moment.

Teacher Toolkit

Reflections!

Tell yourself:
   If you're not making room for play, *you're in the way.*

7

So You're Uncomfortable

There is something really important that we need to talk about before we get to the end of this book—our own discomfort. This is something that we will all deal with at one time or another in our practice. How many times have you watched the children do something and just cringed because it made you uncomfortable? Whether that is them play fighting, climbing a tree, using a material in a way you think is wrong, or choosing to do something that you do not agree with. I know I have! A lot of times, we end up stopping or interrupting a child's play for no other reason than it is making us uncomfortable.

> *Just because something is making you as the adult uncomfortable does not mean that it is not something that is developmentally informed and responsive.*

This leads us to something I like to call "rethinking our 'no'." So often when I visit childcare programs, I hear the word "no" many more times than I would like to. Sometimes I hear a "no" in words and sometimes I hear it in actions. But either way, it always gives me pause and makes me come back to this idea of what it means to "rethink our 'no'." Let's dissect what I mean:

DOI: 10.4324/9781032679808-8

Rethinking Your "No"

Let's say that you see a child climbing a tree while you are out-side. They are climbing higher and higher. They seem to be enjoying themselves very much and call you over to watch them climb. At first glance, you are immediately anxious and nervous that the child will fall from the tree and break their leg, so you begin the process of telling them to get down and not to climb the tree that high or at all. Here is a great space to begin the pro-cess of rethinking your no. Try this:

| take a pause and reflect on why it is you want them to stop what they are doing.

| decide if the reason is based in safety or a legitimate concern or based solely on your own discomfort.

| if the reason is a safety concern, let the child know this and have a conversation with them about why.

| if the reason is your own discomfort, share that with the child as well. Let them know that you are a little uncomfortable with what they are doing right now, and you want to check in with them.

| check in with them and ask them how they are feeling. Do they feel safe? Do they need anything from you to feel safer? Remind them that you are there if they need you.

| continue to observe the child and offer assistance when necessary or requested.

We can apply the same process when we are talking about children and weapon play. A lot of the time with weapon play in particular, our "no" is coming from our own discomfort with the idea of this play. Whether that is from our own experiences with weapons, or our fear of being reprimanded for allowing the children to play this way, it is almost always from our own feelings. So we can reflect and make our decisions based on those reflections.

Something that really helped me with the idea of weapon play (because I was the teacher who would say "no" automatic-ally whenever I saw children in weapon play) was to reflect back on our classroom agreements that I told you about at the begin-ning of this book.

| i am kind to myself
    | i am kind to others
    | i am kind to the environment

I would remind myself of those agreements and think, is what the children doing aligned with those agreements? If not, we can have a conversation about it. But if it is aligned, then why am I saying no? These are the agreements we came up with together, right? So why am I not following them myself? That was a really great way for me to remind myself to reflect and think about my "no."

Remember that in my conversations with the children in which we created these agreements, we also discussed the issues surrounding this type of play, our feelings about it, kindness, consent, etc. So, all of that is also tied into the reflection I was doing when I wanted to say no. If you have already decided (either with the children or not) that weapon play is not something that is appropriate for your program—you can still use the same reflection techniques with your no's. You can still have conversations with the children about why this is not appropriate. You can also use this technique when it comes to other activities that the children may be doing that are causing you anxiety or discomfort.

The thing I want you to remember the most out of all this talk about reflection and rethinking is:

You have to be open to having honest conversations with the children. Period.

No matter what it is that you are deciding to do regarding weapon play, no matter what it is that the children are doing that is making you uncomfortable, no matter how you are feeling, no matter your experiences, no matter what having conversations with the children that are open, honest, truthful, and often is the absolute best thing you could do. Not only does this create a mutually respectful and beneficial relationship between you and the children, it also shows them that they matter, that the thoughts they have and the words they say have meaning and encourages them to speak up for themselves.

Remember what I said previously about our work being a way to heal ourselves and our inner child? That is also what conversations can do. A lot of us were not encouraged to have conversations like this when we were children. We were not encouraged to speak up—especially to adults, right? So when we make that shift with our children now, we can also give our inner child something that it has been seeking as well.

The bottom line is this: just because something makes you uncomfortable does not mean that you have to say no to it. Just because something that the children are doing is waking up some feelings of discomfort or trauma for you does not mean that what they are doing is not developmentally informed and responsive. We need to be able to reflect on ensuring that we are coming to our work with the children without those feelings of bias clouding our judgment.

> It is not about you. It is not about us. It is about the children.

So, what can you do in your practice to rethink your no? What are some things that cause you anxiety or discomfort that the children do (weapon play or not) and how can you use this technique to think differently about your no?

8

The Importance of Connection

As we get to the end of this book, we want to make sure that we talk about something that is a huge piece of our work—our connection to each other.

As we have talked throughout this book, many feelings may have come up. And feelings may have come up from those feelings and so on. The work that we do comes with a lot of baggage. It is very intimate work that we do. We work closely with children and their families. We get to know them on an extremely personal level. We learn about them. We connect with them. That is what makes our work different from most careers—we make true connections each day that stay with us and (hopefully) them long after our time together is done. It is one of the most beautiful things about the work that we do. A lot of times it is one of the things that keep us working and that keeps us going. Because the connections we make with the children and families and being able to continue to see them grow after they leave us through social media or friendships are so meaningful.

However, as wonderful as all of this can be in our practice, we also know that it can come with a lot of not-so-great things too. Our work is stressful, overwhelming, thankless, exhausting, scary, and so many other emotions that we may feel all in one day! It is something specific to what we do that no one can really understand unless they have experienced it themselves. That is why being able to connect to each other is so paramount. There is

DOI: 10.4324/9781032679808-9

something special about connecting with others in the field and being able to share our struggles and our celebrations together. It is something that has made a huge positive impact on me and my practice—as well as my own mental health.

Sometimes in our work, not only can it be difficult on a base level due to the reasons we have discussed but it can be even more difficult or lonely when we begin to rethink our practice. When we start to open our minds more to what is really important for children or what it is that we really want for them to experience, it can sometimes become lonely because (as I am sure you know) many adults do not view children in the same way. The overarching idea about children and childhood is still basically the same children should behave, listen, do as they are told, do good in school, and get a good job. When we begin to self-reflect and begin to change our own thoughts and ideas about children and what is truly developmentally informed and responsive, many people we work with may find that upsetting because they have yet to rethink their own practice. This is even more of a reason that we need to find our community—a group of educators who are doing the work as well and who we can collaborate with, support, and encourage.

Do you ever feel alone in your practice? I know I definitely did. I was always known as the "crazy teacher" (sidenote, I do not use that word normally and have shifted my language to be more inclusive, but for the point of this story, that is what they called me) because I allowed the children to be who they were. Because I had open and honest conversations with the children. Because I truly respected who they were, what they thought, and what they had to say. Being able to give children a space like that is extremely rewarding, but it can definitely be lonely. Well, if this is you and you understand what I am talking about, we are here for you! We don't just want this book to be a resource for you when it comes to self-reflection, weapon play, and consent, but we want this book to be a way for all of us to connect with each other and not only help support and strengthen each other's practice but also strengthen our own.

We are amazing on our own, but we are even better together.

We have created a community space just for you. A space where you can come together and find folx who are going through exactly what you are going through. Folx who know exactly how it feels to be where you are. Folx who can support you and you can support in return. Finding and building community in our practice has been one of the most rewarding things I have ever done or been a part of, and I hope that you will take this chance to check it out. You can find the community on my website, honoringchildhood.org, or by searching "Honoring Childhood: The Community" on Facebook.

We encourage you to use this space as you see fit. You can connect with others who have read and gone through this book and discuss your thoughts and ideas that came from it, or you can just connect with an amazing group of educators already there about your practice and your struggles and celebrations. We hope you find community here—and we will be there too!

9

Resources

Books

For the reflective lean in:
   Think Again: The Power of Knowing What you don't know, Adam Grant
For the renegade:
   It's Okay Not to Share, Heather Shumaker
For the mystic:
   The Alchemist
For the one who wants to learn, but also wants to laugh:
   Permission to Screw Up, Kristen Hadeed
For the culturally responsive:
   Unearthing Joy, Ghouldy Muhammad

Podcasts

Honoring Childhood, Samuel Broaden
That Early Childhood Nerd, Heather Bernt-Santy
The Powerful Pedagogy, w/ Lynnette Arthur
Defending the Early Years w/ Kisha Reid
Raising Wildlings w/ Nicci & Vicci

DOI: 10.4324/9781032679808-10

Instagram

Kisa: @iam_still_learning and Samuel: @honoringchildhood
Annie and Candis: @livingoutofline
Chazz Lewis: @mrchazz

The Book Table

Like many, as a child I relied on my imagination as a sanctuary from all the big and scary things in my world. Whether I was drawing about children who were unwanted by family or friends, creating epic, *Lord of the Flies*-style dramas with the silverware at my kitchen sink, or stowing away with Henry, Jessie, Violet, and Benny in my favorite childhood book, *The Boxcar Children*. The recesses of my mind made the perfect playscape, and through my imaginative adventures, I was able to safely explore concepts that were too big or too frightening to give a voice to. Below you will find a few early childhood books that provide mirrors, windows, and recess for children who play freely in their mind.

Trauma
The Invisible String, Patrice Karst
I See You
The Queen on our Corner
The Tunnel
Something Terrible Happened
The Fox and *The Forest Fire*
Up and Down
Bird
To the Other Side
My Brother Is Away

Scary Times
Goggles, Ezra Jack Keates
Homeland
Idriss and His Marble

Sarah Rising
Mama's Nightingale
The Talk
One Thursday Afternoon
Something Happened in Our Park

War/Conflict

Until Someone Listens
War
The Day War Came, Nicola Davies
Migrants, Issa Watanabe
Cape, Kevin Johnson
I'll Be the Moon, Phillip D. Cortez
The Little Green Jacket, Jodi Dee
Nonni's Moon, Julia Inserro
From the Stars to the Sea, Tarah Schneberger

Death

The Memory Box, Joanna Rowland
The Grief Rock
A Garden of Creatures
The Scar
The Boy and the Gorilla
Missing Mommy
A Shelter of Sadness
The Longest Letsgoboy
The Phone Booth in Mr. Hirota's Garden

10

Final Reflections and Your Monday Morning Moment of Truth

We know that this book and the things we discussed throughout can be heavy and difficult to work through, but we want to end this book by saying that we are PROUD of you! We are proud of you for taking this step in your practice and for doing the self-reflective work needed in our work. It is not an easy thing to do—believe us, we know!

We also want to take this time to collect some final reflections for you to consider as you move forward in your practice and your life:

1. Please remember the goal that we set for you and this book at the very beginning. It wasn't to change your mind about weapon play. It wasn't to have you go back to your program tomorrow and give all the children play guns and sticks and tell them to shoot and fight each other. Our goal was and is still for you to think differently about this type of play and learn how to use self-reflection to think differently about not only this type of play but you and your practice itself. So, whether you are at the end of this book and going forward to bring more weapon play into

DOI: 10.4324/9781032679808-11

your practice or if you are leaving this book with more conversations to have with the children and folx you work with, you did it! Remember, no one knows your community or your practice more than you do.

2. The world is a scary place—both for children and for us. Remember that it is equally important that we give ourselves space for reflection, self-care, meditation, and more as much as we do for the children and families that we serve. Connection to each other in this work is paramount. We need each other now more than ever. So, reach out, you are not in this alone and you don't have to be. Our work, while rewarding and beautiful, can also be very hard, stressful, lonely, and thankless. It is hard for anyone to understand that unless they are in our shoes. So, reach out to each other—reach out to us. Another goal that we had with this book was bringing folx together to support and encourage each other not just with the idea of weapon play but with our practice as a whole.

3. You and your experiences matter! Everything that you have been through in your life, everything that you do and believe about children and the work you do, everything you are matters, is important, and has value to the people around you and our world. Don't ever forget that.

4. It is ok to be uncomfortable! This is something that I really needed to work on myself because it is not fun to be uncomfortable, right? But when we are uncomfortable, a lot of times, we are right where we need to be. So, celebrate that discomfort and lean into it. You may find out more about yourself than you thought.

5. Conversation is everything! We should have played a game to count how many times I wrote the word "conversation" in this book because it is my favorite word! But that is because it is so important in the work that we do. How are you going to bring more conversations into your classroom or program and how are you going to use those conversations to create a safe and supportive space for yourself and the children?

6. You are doing a great job! I always like to end my books, trainings, talks, etc., with this. Our job can be very thankless at times. But we are here to tell you that we see you, we hear you, and we are with you. And we believe in you and all that you are doing! We know that sometimes it can feel that we are not doing a good job at all. We come home and think about a hundred things we should have or could have done differently and that can make us feel discouraged. But remember, the fact that you are trying to do all you can to create the best environment and experience for the children you serve means you are doing a great job. The impact you are having on these children today will carry with them and help to create a better and kinder world for us all. So, thank you!

Now, it is time to figure out what you are going to do with all that you learned and reflected on throughout this book. That's right, it is time to reflect and create your Action Plan and Monday Morning Moment of Truth. Use the space provided below to write out your goals for your program and your classroom as it relates to what you learned and reflected on in this book. Remember, you can come back to this and update/change your goals as time goes on. This field is constantly changing and evolving, and we should be doing the same thing. And remember, be honest with yourself! What is it that you want to take back into your practice from this book? What spoke to you? What challenged you? What surprised you? Let it all out!

Reflections!

Alright, you make it to the final page of this book on a Friday night and have the whole weekend to process the stories within. You're hopeful and believe that you are capable of doing the hard things necessary to allow space for play styles that you once were either afraid of or flat-out against. You walk into your learning space on Monday morning, turn on the lights (or greet everyone outside if you have outdoor learning), and then what?

You wait for the opportunity to present itself. As Samuel said, you're not going to be whittling a tiny arsenal out of every fallen branch you find during your nature walk. When a child asks you to play a game with them, you aren't going to hand them the foam sword and suggest that they kill you, and you aren't going to start taking bets on the children and start a fight club on your preschool playground. The groundwork has been laid, that was the hard part. Now all you need to do is let the play unfold naturally. Your Monday Morning Moment of Truth may very well be on Tuesday before nap or on a Friday before time to go home, but it will happen so be prepared.

Your Monday Morning Moment of Truth is your commitment to gradually shifting your mindset. Every day is a new opportunity to stretch yourself, reconsider, and reimagine. And every day, like Monday morning, is a clean slate, a time to reflect on where you are in your journey, rejoice over the moments when you catch yourself leaning into the change, and repair things that didn't go the way that you planned.

Whether you overhear a conversation about death play without feeling the urge to intervene, observe children involved in rough-and-tumble play and consider the benefits before worrying about intention, liability, or what others may think, or you see a child engrossed in superhero play and know that they are exploring power, you are growing in your practice and that is something to be celebrated. But that's not it. The real magic will reveal itself when the children you work with no longer have to hide their pretend weapons behind their backs in fear that they will be reprimanded. When those children no longer have to create euphemisms to soften the way that *you* are interpreting their play, and when you hear them setting ground rules about how to treat one another, giving or refusing consent, and self-advocating; When there is no need to mask the fact that they are still trying to figure out this complex world we live in, and that is okay, is when you realize that you have created another level of belonging in your environment where thoughts, actions, feelings, and processes are honored. And that, my friend, will be the markers of true success. So, get ready, Monday morning is coming. I'm rooting for you.

> We see you. We hear you. We're with you. We are proud of you.
>
> Samuel and Kisa

Acknowledgments

From Samuel

I truly hope that you gained something from this journey with us. I hope that you were able to think deeper about yourself and your practice. I hope that you feel more confident and prepared to go forward and continue giving children the best you can. Please reach out to us and let's connect more on this idea. I love talking about all things childhood, and I love gaining new connections and relationships with others who view childhood in this way as well. Thank you for joining me on this journey, I am so honored to have shared this space with you.

Weapon play is something that I have become very passionate about in the last few years of my practice, and I would be remiss to not thank the program I was working at when my thought process began to shift for allowing me to explore new play ideas without judgment or fear of backlash. The program that allowed me to explore these things with the children and that allowed me to create a space for children that I had always wanted. The program that gave me the best year of my practice (and where the amazing children that were a part of the conversation I spoke about a lot in this book attended)!

I cannot believe this is my second book! It has been a lifelong dream of mine to do this, and now I have done it twice! I am living proof that your dreams can come true and you can do it! It is quite a surreal experience, and I would not be able to do any of this without the following people:

I first need to thank my editor Alexis and the entire team at Routledge. From the moment I met Alexis, her enthusiasm for my writing and the thoughts that I wanted to put out into the world was palpable, and I could not wait to work with her. She and the entire team at Routledge have made this journey such a wonderful experience for me, and I could not be more grateful. I am so glad that our paths crossed, and I will forever be grateful to her for helping my dream become a reality.

To my friends who not only supported my dreams but also spent so much of their own time reading and rereading my work, giving me suggestions, and pushing me when I felt like giving up:

Kylie, I don't know what I would do without you. Your constant support and encouragement is unmatched, and I am so thankful that our paths crossed—can you believe we did it?—again.

Megan, Emily, Tonya, Estera, Nancy, Kim, Laura, and all of #TeamOregon, I love you all so much and am so grateful for our friendship and how we have become so close. My girls, can you believe it?

Ra-Sha-homie, look at this! I did it! I don't know what I would have done without you in my life all these years. I cherish our friendship and am so grateful for all you have done and continue to do for me. Look how far we have come!

Tia—my ride or die. We have long since moved beyond friends to becoming a true family. I love you so much and cannot wait to celebrate this second book with you! Love you forever.

To my girl, my sis Ron Grady-girl, I love you so much! Who would have thought that me chasing you down at a conference to meet you would have led us to where we are now! I am so thankful for you, our friendship, and where we are. Let's continue to conquer the world! Not we're legit authors girl!

To my queen, my mom Jennifer. I would not be the person I am today without you. I love you so much, and as always, this is for you!

To my boys—Oliver, Baby Bear, and Moon—daddy loves you!

To my world, my best friend, my business partner, my husband Perry. I love you more than words can express. I am so grateful to have found you and to be going on this journey of life with you by my side. There is no other way that I would have it. What team do we play for?!

And a HUGE thank you and a lifetime of gratitude to my amazing friend and co-author Kisa Marx—I always knew we had a special connection and I am so blessed to have been able to go on this journey with you. I am so proud of you, and all you have done and cannot wait to see where this takes you! Family for life!

And thank you to YOU! Thank you for reading this book. Thank you for doing the work. Thank you for trusting yourself. Thank you for honoring me by reading my words. You have no idea how much you mean to me.

From Kisa

I cannot begin to express the tremendous gratitude that I carry to anyone who ventures to read this book. It was a testament to our commitment to the work of honoring childhood, a way to amplify the voices of children, and a love letter to the inner child that has found safety, honor, and a voice within each of us. I hope that our dedication to the children that we serve as well as our fellow educators, practitioners, providers, caregivers, careworkers, or whatever title you give to the important work you do, comes through on the page.

To Samuel, I'd love to say who knew I'd be writing the acknowledgments to a book I'd written with the human I listened to as a fan, just two short years ago? The answer is me. I knew! I'm only half joking because I didn't know what we would do together, but I knew that we were destined to meet, that we shared a passion for too many of the same things not to vibe, and I knew, without a shadow of a doubt that the moment we connected, the sky was the limit. So, thank you. Thank you for reading the message I sent to your inbox and receiving it with an open heart. Thank you for listening to me without judgment; providing counsel; introducing and being willing to share my now Baby Bro, Perry with me; and trusting me to embark on this journey with you and giving me space to be autonomous. You have etched your imprint on my heart, and it can never be erased.

To My Mama, who we all affectionately call Tee. I wouldn't be here if not for you. Not in ability and not in physical form. It goes without saying that I am grateful to you for bringing me into the world (also, you're welcome, lol). I am grateful that you always made space for me to be me. You never asked me to be less or do more. The awkward, anxious, dorky, overimaginative me was always enough. But what I am most grateful for is your gift of story. From indulging my childhood curiosity by retelling the "grown-up" books you were reading, the family folklore and ghost tales, to the first time you read us your written work, I knew with all my heart that what you were doing, I wanted to do. Now, look at us—both writing words for a living. Words don't mean much to a lot of people, but it means everything to us, and I am so grateful to have inherited that gift from you. Also, thanks for always seeing the things in me that I couldn't see and telling me even when I refused to listen.

To Barry, you are a beacon of light. You entered our lives 30 years ago in such an unassuming way, and quietly, carefully, you have become our family's anchor. You adored my mother, accepted all of us through our growing pains and celebrated our successes. You have been an incredible grandfather, and I don't know where any of us would be without you.

To my big brothers, the people responsible for the self-confidence that I possess. You two always made me feel like I was capable of anything. I was worth defending, worth talking to, and worth being inconvenienced for. You wrote the blueprint for how I treat the children that I care for. I know the difference belonging makes in building someone who won't fold even in the midst of adversity, and I thank you for pouring into me without condition.

Steve, my first superhero, the first person to ever make me feel safe, and the first person to celebrate my weirdness out loud, and to date, the word "nerd" still makes me feel warm and fuzzy. You were also the first person to introduce me to the art of narrative. Your teenage tales of what you did when you were out "on a mission" are epic and still play in my heart and mind.

Ceejay, thank you for testing out your rap lyrics on me, giving me my rap name, (Special K), and introducing me to my love of hip-hop. Also thank you for pushing me while remaining gentle. It's a delicate balance that is lost on many, but I'd like to think that I have the grit that I do, not as a trauma response but because someone taught me how to persevere with grace. I can be calm and easy natured and uneffwithable at the same time, just like a well-trained baby bull.

To my twin, my RaMie. Whether you're gliding against my breeze, or you're providing the wind beneath my wings, you will always be the other half of me. Remember, when we were kids and you said people were going to watch you doing what you do every day and I said I was gonna write about it. Look at us, doing what we said we were gonna do! You are who I always knew you would be, and I love to see you living in your light. Love you forever and always, your Sybil Sadie.

To Big Chris, babe, I talk smack about my magic often—how I am living the dreams I spoke into existence. What I don't mention is the architect behind my alchemy. Who I am now is who you knew I would be if I went into business. The connections I've made are proof positive of what you said would happen if I "went outside," and I'm wrapping up the book you said would never get written as long as my words stayed above the refrigerator. You always see the best in me and forgive my worst, and if there's a life without you as my partner, well, it's a life I don't want. You're stuck with me, and I wouldn't have it any other way. Love, Keeza

To the three incredible souls that caught a ride earthside through me: thank you for choosing me. Each of you has brought value and joy into my lives, and though you are all adults, my wish for you is still the same: that you know joy, always have enough to eat, and a good night's sleep.

Shyheim, you made parenting easy, which was a gift for parents with no skills. I often think of the things I do well having learned through doing them incorrectly with you, but you have always shown me compassion and grace, and it hasn't gone unnoticed. Thank you for being the incredible human that you are—your soul is gold and everyone who knows you, present company included, is better for it.

Christopher, your heart drives the purpose in what I do. Everything I wish had been provided for you, and poured into you, and forgiven of you, is what I aim to provide for children that I come across who remind me of you. Though I wish I could change your past, I can't. But I can be sure as hell work hard enough to meet you where you are now with all the love, support, and grace you deserve. Your growth has not gone unnoticed. Keep going and keep growing. I see you, we all do, and I hope you see it too.

Jalen, Jay, my neach. You are the manifestation of your parents' growth: strong, determined, and proud. You embrace your imperfections and are continuously striving to improve. You are empathetic, gentle, and kind. A loyal little brother and a trusted friend. I know life hasn't been easy, but we create the change we want to see. Chin up. Eyes on the prize. I can't wait to see what you dream up.

Love you all to infinity and beyond, Ma

Printed in Great Britain
by Amazon

43785192R10064